SUPER SCANNING TECHNIQUES

TECHNIQUES

The Hewlett-Packard Guide to
Black-and-White Imaging

Jerry B. Day

RANDOM HOUSE
ELECTRONIC PUBLISHING

New York

Published in the United States by Random House, Inc., New York, and simultaneously in Canada by Random House of Canada, Ltd.

Manufactured in the United States of America.

12345678910

First Edition

Library of Congress Cataloging-in-Publication Data

Day, Jerry, 1940-

       Super Scanning Techniques / by Jerry B. Day.

       p. cm.

       Includes references and index.

       ISBN 0-679-75157-2 : $24.00

Trademarks

Microsoft®, Microsoft Word for Windows™, and Microsoft Windows™ are trademarks of Microsoft Corporation.

Adobe® Photoshop™, Adobe Illustrator™, and Adobe Streamline™ are trademarks of Adobe Systems, Inc. Postscript® is a registered trademark of Adobe Systems, Inc. in the U.S. and other countries.

Linotronic™ is a trademark of Allied Corp.

AutoCAD™ is a trademark of Autodesk Inc.

Macintosh® is a registered trademark of Apple Computer.

Ventura Publisher® is a registered trademark of Corel Systems Corporation.

CorelDRAW™ and Corel TRACE™ are trademarks of Corel Systems Corporation.

Hijaak™ is a trademark of Inset Systems.

PhotoFinish™ is a trademark of ZSoft Corporation.

A number of entered words in which we have reason to believe trademark, service mark, or other proprietary rights may exist have been designated as such by use of initial capitalization. However, no attempt has been made to designate as trademarks or service marks all personal computer words or terms in which proprietary rights might exist. The inclusion, exclusion or definition of a word or term is not intended to affect, or to express any judgment on, the validity or legal status of any proprietary right which may be claimed in that word or term.

DEDICATION

To Anne, my wife for thirty wonderful, exciting years.
You are truly the wind beneath my wings!

ACKNOWLEDGMENTS

I would like to thank all of the many individuals who contributed to this book in so many ways. Thanks to everyone at Hewlett-Packard's Greeley Hardcopy Division who took time from their busy schedules to make sure everything is technically correct (any errors or mistakes are mine and not theirs). Thanks to the thousands of wonderful folks who use HP ScanJet scanners to produce so many exciting and interesting projects—they provided the inspiration to produce this book. Particular thanks to Ronald Musto of *Italica Press,* Ray Ostile of Capstone Electronics, and John Parker of San Juan Car Company for sharing their interesting and creative work with all of us. Thanks to all of the people and companies who so freely and willingly provided information and products necessary to complete this book. Particular thanks to Laura Ducoff of Adobe Systems Inc. for her support and encouragement. Special thanks to Tracy Smith, Mia McCroskey, and all of the staff at Random House who were involved in producing *Super Scanning Techniques.*

INTRODUCTION

As the price of color desktop printers decreases and the quality of desktop color printing increases, more business and technical publications will be printed in color. But, for the immediate future, most business and technical publishing will be in black and white. There continues to be a need for high-quality black-and-white images. *Super Scanning Techniques* provides information on scanning drawings and photographs in black-and-white. This book is designed to be a supplement to the user guides that accompany each Hewlett-Packard ScanJet scanner. You should read the appropriate HP ScanJet scanner user documentation before using this book as you will need to know the basic features of your HP ScanJet scanner and the DeskScan II software. This book provides information applicable to HP ScanJet scanners that support the HP DeskScan II software. The material is applicable to both Apple Macintosh computers as well as computers using Microsoft Windows.

Super Scanning Techniques is intended to provide instructions, information, and tips to help you to be productive and creative with your HP ScanJet scanner. I hope that this book also provides information that will show you how to have fun with it!

In this Book

This book shows you how to get more from your HP ScanJet scanner and how to use it in ways you may not have thought of.

Chapter 1 "How Scanning Works" describes what a scanner is, how one works, and illustrates what you can do with a scanner.

Chapter 2 "Selecting an Image Type" explains how to select an image type for your scanned images.

Chapter 3 "Selecting a File Format" describes the various file format types and explains how to select one of the formats for your images.

Chapter 4 "Getting the Best Scan" explains how to use the DeskScan II tools and controls to produce the best scanned image.

Chapter 5 "Using Scanned Images with Software Applicatgions" provides information on how to use your scanned images with software applications such as word processing, image editors, etc.

Chapter 6 "Tracing" describes the process of converting bitmapped images to a vector format by using tracing software.

Chapter 7 "Scanning Tips & Techniques" provides a selection of tips and tricks to help you be more productive and have fun with your scanner.

Chapter 8 "Printing Scanned Images" explains how to print your scanned images.

Chapter 9 "Real World Scanning" illustrates actual projects produced by real people with their HP ScanJets.

Chapter 10 "References" lists books, magazines, and clip art that will help you get more from your scanner.

Contents

CHAPTER

I

HOW SCANNING WORKS

Introduction

As you don't have to know how a car works in order to drive one, you don't need to know how a scanner works to use one. However, knowing how a car works will make you a better, safer driver because you will understand some of the capabilities (and limitations) of the vehicle. Knowing a bit about the inner workings of your HP ScanJet scanner will help you understand its capabilities and give you an appreciation of what is happening when you scan that drawing or photograph.

What Is a Scanner?

Your Hewlett-Packard ScanJet scanner is similar in function to the familiar office copy machine. It may also be thought of as a form of electronic camera. You may think of it as a "magic picture machine" or as the device that gives your computer eyes. Your HP ScanJet is classified as a desktop flatbed scanner. There are several types of scanners available, ranging from low-resolution hand-held devices to ultra-high resolution drum scanners. Your HP ScanJet was designed for many mid-range scanning needs and requirements ranging from the production of school and church newsletters to four-color publications such as magazines.

Scanners are used to scan photographs, drawings, sketches, blueprints, clip art, logos, etc. With the addition of optical character recognition (OCR) software, they can convert text printed on a page to electronic text that can be edited in text editors and word processors.

Hewlett-Packard ScanJet IIp mono-chrome 300 dpi scanner.

Hewlett-Packard ScanJet IIcx color and monochrome 400 dpi scanner.

How Does a Scanner Work?

A Scanner Works Somewhat Like a Camera

The best way to understand how a scanner works is to compare it to a photographic camera. Comparing a scanner to an office copy machine is not the best analogy as the copy machine cannot store the image it is copying as does a camera—and a scanner! A scanner and a camera both have lenses and they record light reflecting from an object. The camera uses photographic film (either negative or positive film) to record images. The scanner records images electronically. A quick review of how a camera works will help in understanding how your HP ScanJet works.

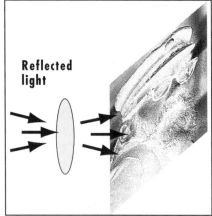

Light passes through a camera's lens and is recorded on the photographic film as a negative image.

© 1978 Jerry B. Day

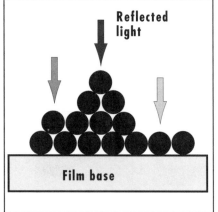

Parts of the photographic film that received more light will actually be thicker than the parts that received less light.

The camera contains a lens to capture the light (for this discussion, we are forgetting the shutter and other parts of the camera). It uses film to record the image. Photographic film consists of an acetate base coated with light-sensitive silver (color films also record images with silver, the silver is converted to color dyes during processing). When the film is exposed, dark areas of the scene reflect small amounts of light and light areas reflect larger amounts of light. When the film is processed, the silver that was exposed is turned black and the silver that was not exposed is removed by the chemicals. So areas that received a lot of light will be darker and those that received less light will be lighter. If you were to examine the negative film under a microscope, you would see that some areas of the film are actually thicker than others.

Scanners Don't Use Film

Your HP ScanJet records light somewhat like a camera. But there are several differences: the scanner does not use film and it has a built-in light source (a lamp). Light from the lamp is reflected from the image to an array of charge-coupled devices (CCDs). These devices are analogous to the film in your camera in that they are light-sensitive. The CCDs detect the amount of light reflecting from each area of the image. Other electronics in the scanner assign a number to each area. These numbers are represented by combinations of one and zeros (called *bits* for binary digits). Computers only understand numbers, so rather than recording the image as varying densities of silver, the scanner records the image as numbers.

Depending on the type of image, your HP ScanJet will scan your originals as a 1-bit, 4-bit, 8-bit, or 24-bit (required for color) image. You might think of *bits* as the silver on photographic film. You have probably have heard the term *bitmap*. A bitmap is a map of where each point of the image (pixel) is and whether it is black, white, or a shade of gray.

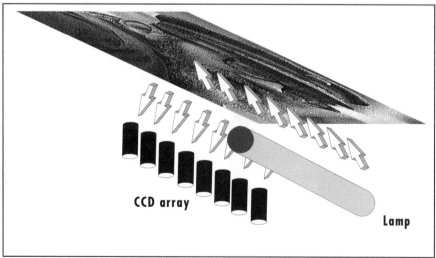

Light projected from the lamp is reflected from the image to the CCD array which records the varying densities as does the film in a camera.

Note

The terms *dots* and *pixels* are often used interchangeably. *Dots-per-inch* is used to describe resolution in both printers and scanners. *Pixels* probably more accurately describe scanning because they include both spatial and tonal information.

The simplest type of bitmap is that of a line art image. Line art consists of drawings, sketches, logos, clipart—anything that is black and white only (no shades of gray). The bitmap of a line art image describes where each point is and whether the dot is black or white. If you were photographing line art with a camera, the film would have only areas with lots of silver and areas with no silver (blank spaces).

Remember how the silver on photographic film is thicker in some areas than others? If you were photographing line art, all areas with silver would have the same depth. As with photographic film, bitmaps have depth. To record a line art image, the bitmap only needs one level of depth, because it is recording black or white only.

Illustration of a bitmap of a line art image. The bitmap has a depth of one bit, hence the term 1-bit image.

To record images that consist of many levels of gray as well as black and white, the raster image (bitmap) must have more than one level of depth. As the silver on photographic film was thicker in some areas than others, a scanned grayscale bitmap image requires more bits in some areas than others. To record greater amounts of information, computers require more numbers as the photographic film requires more silver. Four bits can record 16 levels of gray. Eight bits (also called a byte) are needed to record the 256 levels of gray required to accurately represent most black-and white photographs.

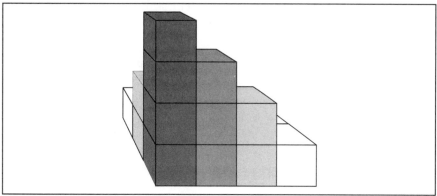

Illustration of pixel depth. Each shade or gray level requires different numbers. For example, white has a different number (or depth) than a light gray, and black has a different number than dark gray.

Keep in mind that *pixel depth* or *bitmap depth* is only a theoretical explanation used to describe the storage of black-and-white and gray scale information. Each dot in a black-and-white line art image is only one bit deep. A 256-level grayscale is 8 bits deep. The numbers between 0 and 255 are levels of gray from white to black. Depth in this case is not an actual physical depth (as is the silver on photograph film), but is an imaginary depth used to describe the numbers used to record different levels of gray. To conclude our brief explanation of how a scanner works, you can see that while it resembles an office copy machine in some ways, it is more like a camera.

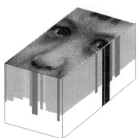

Photo film records images with varying levels of silver—scanners record images with different numbers (bits).

© 1978 Jerry B. Day

What Can You Do with a Scanner?

If you are reading this book after learning to use your HP ScanJet with the user guides, you already know some of the things you can do with a scanner.

- Scan photographs

   Everyone likes to see photographs in publications. We live in a visual age. Photographs are perceived as reality. Photographs in a document provide a feeling of authenticity and authority. Adding photographs to publications was (in the past) an art reserved for paste-up artists and graphic art studios. Today, with your HP ScanJet scanner, a laser printer, and scanning software, you can easily include photographs in your documents and publications.

Scanned as 256-level grayscale at 200 dpi and saved as an Encapsulated PostScript (EPS) file.
© 1977 Jerry B. Day

- Scan line art
  Line art is black-and-white only art work such as drawings, company or department logos, cartoons, charts, etc. Line art is a particularly effective form of visual communication for newsletters, technical publications, training literature, reports, etc.—any publication that may be produced with a laser printer and duplicated with an office copy machine or quick print duplication.

© 1990 Dynamic Graphics

- **Scan line art and photographs for tracing**
  In addition to scanning line art for direct inclusion in your publications, you can scan line art and photographs for conversion to a vector graphics format that can be used by illustration programs such as Adobe Illustrator, CorelDRAW, or by computer-aided-drafting programs such as AutoCAD and DrafixCAD. Artists, engineers, and crafts people are using this exciting technology to restore historic drawings and to convert paper drawings to digital images.

Illustration produced by:
❶
tracing a photograph with tracing paper
❷
scanning the paper tracing
❸
tracing the scanned image with Adobe Streamline, and
❹
adding details with CorelDRAW. © 1992 Jerry B. Day

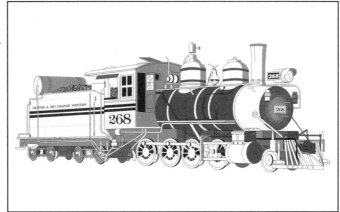

● Scanning for the computer screen

An increasingly popular use of scanners is to scan images for use directly on the computer screen with software applications such as presentations, multimedia, hypertext, training and educational programs, online documentation, etc. Such programs require a variety and large numbers of images and your HP ScanJet is the vehicle for bringing them in. It becomes the eyes of your computer.

See Also

Refer to page 214 for a list of presentation software applications that work with your HP ScanJet scanner.

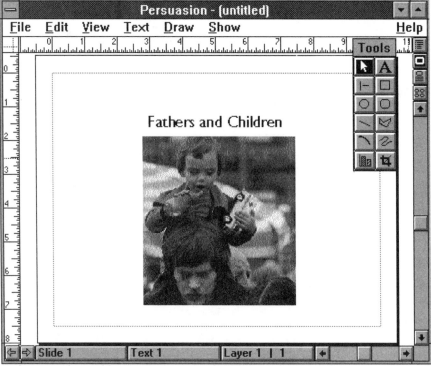

Software such as Aldus Persuasion, CorelSHOW, and Microsoft Powerpoint can be used to produce computer-screen presentations. Scanned images can be incorporated into these presentations in the form of photographs or line art.

© 1977 Jerry B. Day

- **Scan text**

  Your HP ScanJet combined with special software is capable of converting scanned text from a bitmapped image into text characters that can be imported into text editors, word processors, and publishing software. This gives you the capability to read text that was not created on a computer—even text written hundreds of years before computers were invented. Text can be scanned from documents printed with commercial printing presses, with laser printers—even with dot matrix printers.

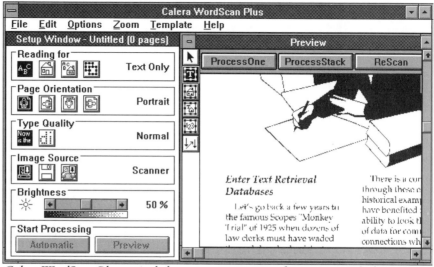

Calera WordScan Plus optical character recognition software is typical of many OCR programs.

A number of optical character recognition software programs are available that will work with your HP ScanJet either on a Macintosh or Windows computer. They all offer a variety of features and capabilities. Some offer the capability of performing optical character recognition directly from your word processor or desktop publishing program. Several OCR programs include special technology (developed by Hewlett-Packard) called AccuPage for enhanced optical character recognition capabilities. Those capabilities include automatically setting of the optimal brightness and removing background colors.

See Also

Refer to page 212 for a list of optical character recognition software applications that work with your HP ScanJet scanner.

CHAPTER

2

SELECTING AN IMAGE TYPE

Introduction

Your HP ScanJet scanner lets you scan an image as one of three image types: drawings, halftone, or grayscale. This chapter will describe and illustrate each image type with examples. The advantages and disadvantages (if any) of each type will be outlined. This chapter will help you to choose the appropriate image type that will produce the best reproduction of your original.

Drawings

Drawings are a HP ScanJet image type that consists of black and white dots (or pixels) only. The original drawings can be pencil sketches, clip art, mechanical drawings, blueprints, etc. Original drawings that have no gray or shaded areas are often called *line art* by designers and graphics professionals. The original line art may be color—that is, black lines or areas may be replaced by green, blue, etc. When scanning in black-and-white, the colored line art is scanned as black dots or white dots. The colored areas are scanned as black dots.

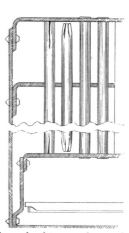

Clip art scanned and traced and saved as a Black and White Drawing image type. The image consists of black areas on a white background.

A black-and-white mechanical drawing scanned and saved as a Black and White Drawing image type.

Your HP ScanJet scanner scans drawings as 1-bit images. Each part of the image is recorded as a pattern of black and white dots. Scanned drawings are referred to as *bi-level* bitmaps because they have only black and white dots—they have a pixel depth of one.

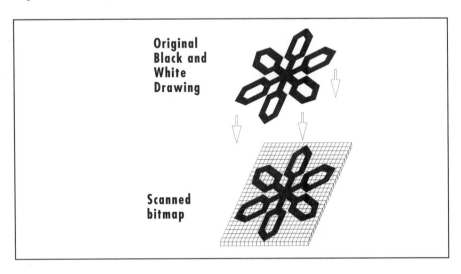

**Original
Black and
White
Drawing**

**Scanned
bitmap**

Halftones

Traditional (Non-Computerized) Halftones

Photographs, paintings, or any image that has a broad range of tones or a gradation of tones is known as *continuous tone*. The broad range of tones is produced in photography by varying the amount of silver or dye in the photograph image. In a painting, the range of tones is produced by varying the amounts of pigment and hue. A problem arises when you wish to print a photograph or painting on a printing press. A offset printing press can print only black ink. It is not capable of printing with varying shades of gray ink. To create the impression of gray, the halftone process was developed. The printed image is produced with dots that vary in size. In dark areas, the dots are large and close together. In lighter areas, the dots are smaller and further apart. Halftone images are an optical illusion—the human eye perceives the pattern of dots as shades of gray.

The image on the right is an enlarged copy of part (the boxed area) of the full image shown below. Note how the dots are grouped to create larger dots that give the illusion of continuous tone.

© 1977 Jerry B. Day

Traditional (non-computerized) halftones are produced by photographing the original photograph or image through a halftone screen onto special graphic arts film. The film is then used to produce a printing plate on metal or plastic. The halftone screens look somewhat like a window screen and are made of glass or film and have a grid of tiny clear dots that act as pinhole lenses. These tiny lenses produce the halftone patterns on the film used to produce the printing plates. The dots on the halftone screens may be square, round, or elliptical. They are arranged in lines at a given number-per-inch referred to as the *screen ruling*. Halftone screens are available in many different screen rulings such as 85 lines-per-inch or 200 lines-per-inch. The higher the number, the finer the screen, and the greater the detail on the printed page.

Traditional (non-computerized) line screens are produced in a variety of line frequencies (lines-per-inch) and dot shapes.

Newspapers are typically printed with 65 to 85 lines-per-inch screens, while high-quality offset magazine or book printers use a 200 lines-per-inch screen. When producing the printing plates, the halftone screen is usually placed at an angle (normally 45 degrees in black-and-white printing) to minimize the appearance of lines. In four-color printing, four halftone screens are used (one screen for black, one for cyan, one for magenta, and one for yellow). Each screen is placed at a different angle to eliminate or minimize the moiré patterns.

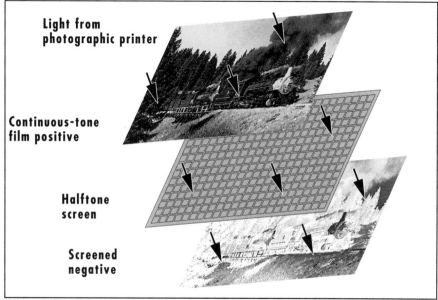

Light from photographic printer

Continuous-tone film positive

Halftone screen

Screened negative

The traditional (non-computerized) halftoning process—a conventional halftone screen is placed between the original continuous-tone image and the graphic art film used to make the screened negative. The screen may be separated from the screened negative or placed in direct contact with it.

© 1971 Jerry B. Day

Before the halftone process was developed, magazines and newspapers used line art to illustrate their pages. The first halftone used in a magazine or newspaper was published in the *New York Daily Graphic* newspaper on March 4, 1880.

Digital Halftones

As publishing evolved into digital production with computers, the same problem that had confronted conventional printers arose. Laser printers and high-resolution devices such as imagesetters can only produce black dots (or in the case of imagesetters, black dots on photographic film or paper). Laser printers and imagesetters have an additional limitation—the dots are all the same size.

Digital halftoning produces the impression of continuous tone by grouping same-size dots into clusters or groups called *halftone cells*. Halftone cells are created by applying a halftone screen. These cells create the impression of larger dots permitting the illusion of continuous tone.

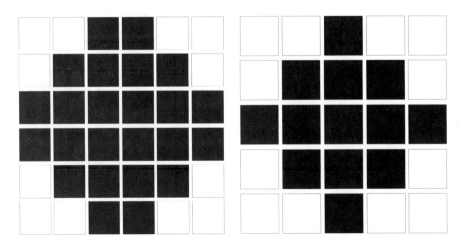

Digital halftone dot produced by grouping laser printer dots into cells, thereby creating the impression of a larger dot.

Halftone dots of different size can be produced by changing the grouping of the laser dots on the grid.

As with conventional halftone screens, digital halftones are produced by varying the halftone frequency (lines-per-inch), the halftone angle, and the halftone dot shape.

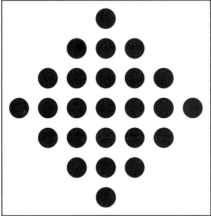

Approximately 60 lines-per-inch, 45-degree angle (typical 300 dpi laser printer)

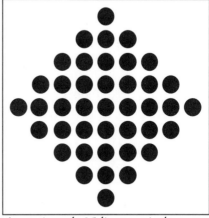

Approximately 85 lines-per-inch, 45-degree angle (typical 600 dpi laser printer)

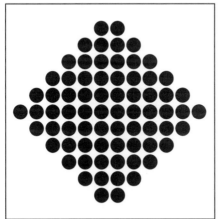

Approximately 125 lines-per-inch, 45-degree angle (typical 1,270-dpi imagesetter)

Digital halftones are produced in one of three ways:

- **The scanner software** includes halftoning capabilities to apply halftoning during scanning
- **The application software** (desktop publishing, image editing, color separation, etc.) typically includes the capability to convert grayscale scanned images to halftones
- **The printer** (PostScript and PCL printers have halftoning capabilities built-in). Grayscale images will be converted to halftones during the printing process.

Your HP ScanJet scanner has the capability to scan your image in one of several halftone modes or patterns. When you scan a continuous-tone image with one of the halftone options, the scanner groups the dots into halftone cells. This process is called *dithering*. The dithering process is the electronic version of photographing an original image through a halftone screen as described beginning on page 17. The halftone screen should be thought of as the pattern that is applied to the dots that create the halftone cells and thus create the impression of gray. No grayscale information is recorded when using halftoning to scan images; the scanned image consists of just black and white dots. Conventional halftone screens are available with different-shaped dots and different frequencies (how far apart the lines of dots will be). In addition, the screens can be rotated to different angles so that the rows of dots can be horizontal, vertical, or any degree in between. Your HP ScanJet scanner's halftoning process uses the electronic version of different halftone screens when scanning images. Six halftone patterns or types are available with your HP DeskScan II software. Each type produces a different pattern of dots. Selecting a halftone pattern involves the type of original, what effect you wish to create, and the type of printer you plan to use for your final output. To help you determine which halftone pattern to use, the DeskScan II software includes a *Samples* option which prints a sample of your image in each of the halftone patterns.

See Also

Refer to page 92 for information on how to use the Samples option.

The halftone patterns available with DeskScan II include:

- Normal

  Use this pattern for images with areas of continuous tones and few details (such as the sky or human faces). This pattern is a compromise between many levels of gray and a fine screen frequency. Use this type when you plan to copy your output with an office copy machine.

Normal Halftone
© 1976 Jerry B. Day

- Fine

  Use this pattern when you wish to have more detail in your images. This pattern does not provide as many gray levels as normal, but gives you greater detail.

Fine Halftone

- **Extra-Fine**
Use this pattern when scanning detailed images such as photographs of landscapes or industrial objects. Images scanned with this halftone pattern do not reproduce well on office copy machines. This pattern does not provide as many gray levels as others, but gives you greater detail.

Extra–Fine Halftone
© 1973 Jerry B. Day

- Horizontal Halftone
This pattern emphasizes vertical detail. Use it on photographs with emphatic vertical lines.

Horizontal Line halftone
© 1978 Jerry B. Day

- **Vertical Line Halftone**

  This pattern emphasizes horizontal detail. Use it on photographs with strong horizontal lines.

Vertical Line Halftone
© 1978 Jerry B. Day

- **Diffusion**

  The Diffusion pattern produces a random dithering. This pattern produces good detail and texture. This pattern minimizes the moiré patterns that can occur when you scan an image that was previously halftoned such as pictures from books, magazines, and newspapers. Images scanned with this pattern do not reproduce well on office copy machines and do not print well on high-resolution imagesetters or commercial printing presses, but do print well on 300- or 600-dpi laser printers.

Diffusion Pattern

Advantage of Scanning Images as Halftones

- The files created by scanning as a halftone are smaller than images scanned as grayscale (the bitmap has no pixel depth as the bitmap consists of black and white dots only).

Disadvantages of Scanning Images as Halftones

- You no longer have the capability of controlling alterations (grayscale scanned images can be enhanced and modified with image editing software and halftones cannot).
- Halftoned images that are enlarged or reduced can produce moiré patterns.
- Halftoned images do not display well on the computer screen because the computer screen has a lower resolution than the halftoned image.

> **Tip:**
> When using one of the halftone patterns, scan for the printer you will use for your final output. Do this even if you are using a lower resolution printer for *proofing*. For example, if you are using a 1,250-dpi imagesetter for your final output, scan your halftones for that device even if you print your proofs on a 300- or 600-dpi laser printer.

Grayscale

You have three image-type options when scanning with your HP ScanJet scanner:

- You can scan drawings (line art) as one-bit bitmaps consisting of only black-and-white dots.
- You can scan using one of the halftoning methods.
- You can scan with 16 or 256 grays.

We have discussed drawings (line art) and halftoning with your HP ScanJet in the first part of this chapter. This part of the chapter discusses grayscale. What is grayscale and why would you want to scan your images as grayscale?

Note

Your HP DeskScan II software image type option defines grayscale images as *Black and White Photo*. When you wish to scan your image as grayscale, select the *Black and White Photo* option.

As discussed previously, laser printers and high-resolution imagesetters produce their images with one size of black dot. They cannot produce continuous tone images with different size dots or by using 256 different gray inks. The impression of continuous tone is created by grouping the same size dots to produce larger halftone dots (sometimes called halftone cells). This process is called halftoning. The halftoning can be produced by the scanner, by software, or by the printer. Your HP ScanJet scanner is capable of capturing your images as halftones or as grayscale images that will be halftoned by the software or by the printer.

In chapter 1, we discussed pixel depth and how your scanner must use data to record levels of gray. HP ScanJet scanners can capture your continuous tone originals as 4-bit images with 16 grays or 8-bit images with 256 grays.

Grayscale Advantages

There are a number of reasons why you should scan your originals as grayscale images:

- Grayscale images can be manipulated, retouched, and enhanced with image-editing or photo-retouching software.

- The contrast and brightness of a grayscale image can be adjusted after it has been scanned with image-editing or photo-retouching software.

Note

You will get better results if the contrast and brightness are correct when the image is scanned versus adjusting the image after the scan is made.

- The screen frequency (lines-per-inch) of grayscale images can be changed and the image printed on higher-resolution printers or imagesetters (for example a grayscale image may be set to 85 lpi for a 600-dpi laser printer and changed to 155 lpi for a 3,000-dpi imagesetter).

- Grayscale images display better on the computer screen. Halftone images can be difficult to see on a computer screen because of the difference in dots-per-inch (72 dpi is typical for a screen versus 200 or 300 for a scanned image).

- Grayscale images will be halftoned at the resolution of the printer you are using (laser printer, imagesetter, etc.).

Extra-fine halftone   *256-level grayscale*

© 1975 Jerry B. Day

Should You Scan at 16-Level or 256-Level?

You have the option with your HP ScanJet scanner of scanning your images as (4-bit) 16-level grayscale or (8-bit) 256-level grayscale. Which should you use and why?

16-level grayscale   *256-level grayscale*

© 1976 Jerry B. Day

Choosing between 16-level grayscale and 256-level grayscale is a trade-off between image quality and file size. How many levels of gray do you need? If the original is a high-contrast photograph with few levels of gray, 16-level grayscale will accurately record the image. If the original is a full continuous tone with many levels of gray, scanning it at 16-level grayscale may result in *posterization* (a high contrast effect created when gray levels are limited) or *banding effects* (banding is the effect of lines or streaks through an image). A 16-level grayscale scan may also tend to look flat (photographer's term for low contrast).

Tip:

With most images, 16 levels of gray will not be enough. Scanning at 256 levels of gray will give you a realistic looking reproduction that has smooth transitions between levels of gray. However, scanning at 256 levels of gray requires more disk storage space. Scanning an 8x10 inch photograph as a 256-level grayscale image at 300 dpi at 100 percent scaling will require more than 5 megabytes of disk space if not compressed. In addition to the disk storage space requirement, image editing or photo retouching a 5-megabyte file requires extra RAM and a fast computer. Your HP ScanJet scanner can compress TIFF files, reducing the disk storage space.

CHAPTER
3

SELECTING A FILE FORMAT

Introduction

This chapter will help you to select a file format when scanning with your HP ScanJet scanner. The factors involved in selecting a file format will be explained. Each file format will be described and the best use of the format explained. The advantages and disadvantages (if any) will be outlined and examples of each file format will be shown.

Input and Output Considerations

When selecting a file format for your scanned images, several questions must be answered:

- Which formats are available for the computer systems I am using?
- Which formats are supported by the applications with which I am using the scanned images?
- What type of printer am I using to produce the document?
- Will the document be duplicated or printed by a commercial printer?

Which Formats Are Available for My Computer?

Not all file formats are available to both Apple Macintosh and MS-DOS/Windows computer systems.

MS-DOS/Windows

When using your HP ScanJet with an MS-DOS system, the following formats can be used:

- TIFF 5.0 and TIFF 5.0 Compressed
- Encapsulated PostScript with or without a screen preview image (EPS)
- PCX
- Windows Bitmap
- OS/2 Bitmap.

Macintosh

When using your HP ScanJet with a Macintosh computer, the following formats can be used:

- TIFF 5.0 and TIFF 5.0 Compressed
- Encapsulated PostScript with or without a screen preview image (EPSF)
- PICT or PICT2
- PICT Compressed
- MacPaint.

Note

Encapsulated PostScript is abbreviated EPS on MS-DOS/Windows computers and EPSF on Macintosh computers.

Which File Formats Work with My Applications?

When selecting a format for your scanned images, you must know which formats are supported by your applications. Not all formats are supported by all applications. For example, the application used to produce this book (Ventura Publisher 4.1) does not support the Windows Bitmap or OS/2 formats. Before scanning an image in a particular format, be sure to check your application to see which formats it supports.

> ### Tip:
> If there were one universal file format for graphics and scanned images it would be TIFF. It works with almost all applications on both Macintosh and MS-DOS computers. It is available on both the Mac and MS-DOS versions of DeskScan II. It works with practically every type of printer from dot matrix to high-resolution imagesetter. It is my recommendation for scanning images.

What Type of Printer Will I Be Using?

Before selecting a file format for your scanned images, you should know that some file formats may not work with your particular printer. For example, Encapsulated PostScript (EPS or EPSF) images can only be printed on a PostScript printer. If you attempt to print a document containing an Encapsulated PostScript image on a non-PostScript printer, either the low-resolution screen image that is a part of EPS files will be printed or no image will be printed.

If you plan to produce your document using a high-resolution imagesetter (such as a Linotronic or Agfa), you may wish to use the Encapsulated PostScript file format.

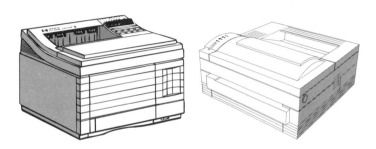

TIFF

What Computers Can It Be Used With?

The TIFF format is available when using your HP ScanJet with either the Macintosh or MS-DOS/Windows version of the DeskScan II software.

What Is It?

TIFF is a file format developed by Aldus and Microsoft in 1986. *TIFF* is an abbreviation of *Tagged Image File Format*. TIFF is used on both MS-DOS and Macintosh systems. TIFF is a bitmapped format capable of storing black-and-white line art, grayscale continuous-tone images, and 24-bit color images. When used on MS-DOS systems, TIFF files have the DOS extension `.tif`. The TIFF format is used to store bitmapped images in paint-type programs and image editors. It is also used to store grayscale screen captures for computer documentation. TIFF and TIFF compressed are two of the formats available to you when scanning with your HP ScanJet scanner.

What Are the Advantages of TIFF?

The TIFF format is the most widely used format for graphic images. It was developed specifically for producing scanned images. Most programs on the MS-DOS and Macintosh systems support the TIFF format, either in the standard or compressed form (many programs support both). TIFF files may be easily moved between computer systems; so TIFF files produced on a Mac may be moved to a PC (or vice versa) with few if any problems. TIFF format images may be produced at any resolution or size and may have any number of levels of gray or colors. TIFF images can be edited or modified by a number of paint programs or image editors. TIFF can be compressed to save disk space, though not all application software can read compressed TIFF files (for example, Ventura Publisher, the program used to produce this book, cannot import TIFF compressed files).

What Are the TIFF Disadvantages?

The TIFF format does have one major limitation or disadvantage: TIFF files are larger than PCX files.

Scanned as 256-level grayscale image and saved in the TIFF format.
© 1978 Jerry B. Day

PostScript (EPS or EPSF)

What Computers Can It Be Used With?

The Encapsulated PostScript format is available when using your HP ScanJet with either the Macintosh or MS-DOS/Windows versions of the DeskScan II software.

What Is It?

PostScript is a page description computer language developed by Adobe and introduced in 1985. The PostScript language is used in laser printers (300 or 600 dpi) and high-resolution imagesetters (1250 to 2450 dpi). Encapsulated Post-Script (EPS) is a graphic file format developed by Adobe for single images. Your HP ScanJet scanner can use the EPS format. When used on MS-DOS systems, Encapsulated PostScript files have the DOS file extension .eps.

What Are the Advantages of PostScript?

PostScript is a vector format, but a PostScript file can include bitmapped images. PostScript is almost a universal format. It is universally used on Macintosh systems and widely used on MS-DOS systems. EPS files can be easily moved from one environment to another (PC to Mac for example). PostScript files are in ASCII format and may be edited by those knowledgeable of the PostScript language (this is not recommended unless you have considerable experience programming in PostScript).

What Are the PostScript Disadvantages?

PostScript files can only be printed to a PostScript printer. Bitmapped images take twice as much disk space in the EPS format than they do in other formats such as TIFF.

Note

The Encapsulated PostScript format may not be a good choice for scanned images because you cannot edit HP ScanJet EPS images with paint programs or image editors. Images can be scanned into image editors or paint programs with TWAIN and saved as EPS.

Encapsulated PostScript files cannot be directly displayed on your Macintosh or PC screen. The only computers that can display PostScript are high-end workstations that use Display PostScript. A PICT file is attached to Macintosh EPSF files for display on your computer screen. A TIFF file is attached to MS-DOS/Windows EPS files and used for screen display. Your HP DeskScan II software gives you the option of saving a Encapsulated PostScript file with or without the PICT or TIFF header. The header makes the file disk space larger. If you choose to save the file without the header, the image will not be displayed on the screen in your application. You will see a large X displayed or a box with data about the file.

Scanned as 256-level grayscale and saved as an Encapsulated PostScript (EPS) file.
© 1977 Jerry B. Day

MacPaint

What Computers Can It Be Used With?

The MacPaint format is available when using your HP ScanJet scanner with the Macintosh version of the DeskScan II software—MacPaint is not available when using your scanner with the MS-DOS/Windows version of DeskScan II.

What Is It?

The MacPaint format takes its name from one of the first programs developed for the Apple Macintosh computer. It was developed as a simple bitmap format for computers with limited memory and disk storage space.

What Are the Advantages of MacPaint?

The MacPaint format is supported by almost all Macintosh applications.

What Are the Disadvantages of MacPaint?

MacPaint images are limited to a maximum size of 720 x 576 dots, a maximum resolution of 72 dots-per-inch and can only be black-and-white line art or halftones (only 1-bit black and white images). You cannot produce a grayscale or color image with the MacPaint format. Not all MS-DOS/Windows programs accept this format. Only use the MacPaint format if you must!

MacPaint images can be a maximum size of 576 dots wide and 720 dots high. If you attempt to scan a larger image, part of it will be automatically cropped. The example on the right was scanned as a Fine Halftone with the Macintosh version of DeskScan II at 72 dpi.

A full view of the photograph shown at top of the page scanned as 256-level grayscale and saved as an EPS file.

© 1978 Jerry B. Day

PICT

What Computers Can It Be Used With?

The PICT format is available when using your HP ScanJet scanner with the Macintosh version of the DeskScan II software—PICT is not available when using your scanner with the MS-DOS/Windows version of DeskScan II.

What Is It?

PICT is an abbreviation of PICTure. Picture was one of the first file formats and was available on the original Macintosh. PICT is part of the Macintosh graphic language. When you use the Macintosh Clipboard, the image is copied in the PICT format. PICT format can be either a vector or bitmap (PICT files produced by your HP ScanJet are always bitmaps). PICT2 is an upgraded, more advanced version of the original PICT standard. PICT2 is the version used by your HP ScanJet.

What Are the Advantages of PICT?

PICT files may be either bitmaps or vector images. Images scanned with your HP ScanJet are always bitmaps. The PICT format imposes no limitations on image resolution. PICT2 files may contain up to 16.8 million colors in the 24-bit form. Almost all Macintosh programs will import PICT images. Some MS-DOS programs can import PICT images (including Ventura Publisher and Aldus PageMaker), but it is not as widely supported on MS-DOS systems as TIFF or EPS. PICT black-and-white images may be colored with an image editor for special effects.

Scanned as a 256-level grayscale image and saved in the PICT format.

© 1980 Jerry B. Day

What Are the Disadvantages of PICT?

The PICT format is widely supported by Macintosh word processing and desktop publishing programs, but the image controls in these programs (such as contrast and brightness) may not work with PICT files. Many imagesetter service bureaus refuse to accept PICT format graphic files because they consider the format to be incompatible with their equipment. If you plan to send your files to an imagesetter (such as a Linotronic or Agfa), check to see if it accepts PICT images or select another file format.

Scanned as a 256-level grayscale image and saved in the PICT format.
© 1977 Jerry B. Day

PICT Compressed

What Computers Can It Be Used With?

Several PICT Compressed formats are available when using your HP ScanJet scanner with the Macintosh version of the DeskScan II software—the PICT Compressed formats are not available when using your scanner with the MS-DOS/Windows version of DeskScan II.

Note

You must install Apple's QuickTime software to use most of the PICT file-compression formats.

What Is It?

Apple's QuickTime software includes file compression programs that allow you to save PICT files in several different compressed formats. Each of these formats offers different levels of image quality, compression ratios, and support by other software programs (such as DTP, word processing, etc.). These formats include:

- **(Apple) Animation**
- **Compact Video**
- **Component Video**
- **(PICT) Graphics**
- **(PICT) None**
- **(PICT) Photo–JPEG**
- **(PICT) Video.**

See Also

Refer to the Apple QuickTime user documentation for information on these formats.

Scanned as a 256-level grayscale image and saved in the PICT Compressed JPEG format.

© 1977 Jerry B. Day

PCX

What Computers Can It Be Used With?

The PCX format is available only when using your HP ScanJet with the MS-DOS/Windows version of the DeskScan II software—it is not available when using your scanner with the Macintosh version of DeskScan II.

What Is It?

The PCX format was created by ZSoft for its PC Paintbrush software. PC Paintbrush is one of the first graphic applications used on MS-DOS systems. PCX files have the DOS file extension `.pcx`.

What Are the Advantages of PCX?

PCX is compatible with virtually all MS-DOS (and Windows) programs. PCX images can be black-and-white, grayscale, or color.

What Are the Disadvantages of PCX?

PCX is primarily a MS-DOS file format. Some Macintosh programs will accept PCX files, but not all. If you plan to exchange files between MS-DOS and Macintosh systems, TIFF or EPS would be a more compatible choice. PCX is not widely supported by service bureaus or used for color separations.

Scanned as a 256-level grayscale PCX file.   © 1976 Jerry B. Day

Windows Bitmap

What Computers Can It Be Used With?

The Windows Bitmap format is available only when using your HP ScanJet with the MS-DOS/Windows version of the DeskScan II software—it is not available when using your scanner with the Macintosh version of DeskScan II.

What Is It?

The Windows Bitmap format was developed by Microsoft for use with MS Windows programs. Windows Bitmap files have the MS-DOS file extension .bmp.

What Are the Advantages of the Windows Bitmap Format?

Windows bitmaps are the standard file format for Microsoft Windows. Windows Bitmaps can be black and white, grayscale, 4-bit, 8-bit, or 24-bit color.

What Are the Disadvantages of the Windows Bitmap Format?

Few non-Windows programs accept Windows Bitmap files. The format is not yet widely used for color separations.

Scanned as a 256-level Windows Bitmap file.

© 1978 Jerry B. Day

OS/2 Bitmap

What Computers Can It Be Used With?

The OS/2 Bitmap format is only available when using your HP ScanJet with the MS-DOS/Windows version of the DeskScan II software—it is not available when using your scanner with the Macintosh version of DeskScan II.

What Is It?

The OS/2 Bitmap format was developed for use with the OS/2 operating system and OS/2 software applications.

What Are the Advantages of OS/2 Bitmaps?

OS/2 Bitmaps are the standard bitmap file format for OS/2. OS/2 bitmaps can be black and white, grayscale, 1-bit, 4-bit, 8-bit, or 24-bit color.

What Are the Disadvantages of OS/2 Bitmaps?

Few (if any) non-OS/2 programs (Macintosh or Windows) accept OS/2 Bitmaps.

Scanned as OS/2 Bitmap, copied to the clipboard, and pasted into this book.
© 1976 Jerry B. Day

File Format Examples

The following examples are the same photograph scanned at 256 levels of gray, at 200 dots-per-inch, and saved in each of the file formats supported by the publishing program used to produce this book. Differences in the images are more related to the way the applications handle the format than the format itself.

Scanned as 256-level grayscale and saved as Encapsulated PostScript (EPS) file.

Scanned as 256-level grayscale and saved as PCX file.

Scanned as 256-level grayscale and saved as TIFF file.

Scanned as 256-level grayscale and saved as Windows Bitmap file.

© 1978 Jerry B. Day

File Size

One very important consideration in choosing a file format to use is how much disk space each format will require. To illustrate the disk space requirements of each format, the same grayscale and line art examples were scanned in each file format. Charts following each example show the file sizes of each format.

Grayscale Example

The photo shown below was scanned as a 256-level grayscale, 200-dpi image in each of the file formats supported by your HP ScanJet (the MacPaint format is 72 dpi and due to the limitations of that format, part of the image was cropped). The chart on the next page shows how much disk space was required to scan this image in each of the file formats.

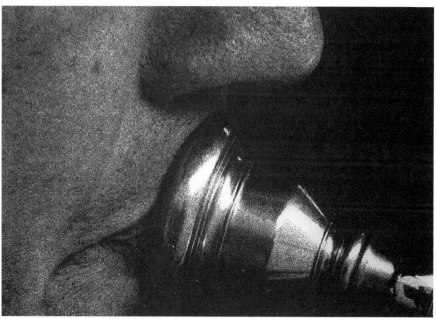

© 1977 Jerry B. Day

Grayscale Example File Format Disk Space Requirements

File Format	File Size (bytes)
TIFF 5.0	610,721
TIFF 5.0 Compressed	536,951
Encapsulated PostScript	1,237,500
Encapsulated PostScript (with screen image)	1,379,691
Windows Bitmap	613,018
OS/2 Bitmap	612,734
PCX	455,238
MacPaint (scanned at 72 dpi)	52,881
PICT	169,282

The chart shows that Encapsulated PostScript with a screen image requires the most disk space of the file formats. It requires approximately 11 times as much disk storage space as the PICT format (which requires the least amount of disk space except for MacPaint which has a maximum resolution of 72 dpi).

Note

The MacPaint file was scanned at 72 dpi (maximum resolution for that format)—all others were scanned at 200 dpi.

Black and White Drawing Example

The following line art example was scanned with the DeskScan II Black and White Drawing option at 300 dpi in each of the file formats supported by your HP ScanJet scanner (the MacPaint format was scanned at 72 dpi and part of the image cropped due to limitations of the format). The chart on the next page shows how much disk space was required to scan this image in each of the file formats.

©Dynamic Graphics

Black and White Drawing Example
File Format Disk Space Requirements

File Format	File Size (bytes)
TIFF 5.0	140,678
TIFF 5.0 Compressed	75,682
Encapsulated PostScript	285,953
Encapsulated PostScript (with screen image)	300,663
Windows Bitmap	140,542
0S/2 Bitmap	140,512
PCX	80,881
MacPaint (scanned at 72 dpi)	28,060
PICT	75,404

As with the grayscale example, the largest file is Encapsulated PostScript with screen image at 300,663 KB and the smallest is the PICT with 75,404 KB (not counting the MacPaint which has a maximum resolution of 72 dpi).

Note

The MacPaint file was scanned at 72 dpi (maximum resolution for that format)—all others were scanned at 300 dpi.

Converting File Formats

If your word processing, desktop publishing, or other application does not support the file format you wish to use with your HP ScanJet, it may be possible to convert the scanned image to a different format. Bitmap paint programs and image editors allow you to import images in one format and save them as a different format. Several file conversion programs are available for both Macintosh and MS-DOS systems that can convert a bitmapped image in one format to a different bitmapped format (TIFF to PCX for example).

To convert a raster image (bitmapped) to a vector image, you must trace the raster image with a tracing program or illustration program with tracing capabilities.

See Also

Refer to chapter 6 for an explanation of the tracing process.

Image imported into Adobe Photoshop as a TIFF file. The Photoshop dodging tools were used to lighten an area of the photograph and the image was exported as an EPS file.

© 1978 Jerry B. Day

Using the Clipboard For File Conversions

The Macintosh and Microsoft Windows Clipboards also offer additional file-format conversion possibilities. You may be able to cut or copy a graphic to the clipboard, paste it into an application and save it in a format that the application supports.

Example of a file conversion using the Microsoft Windows Clipboard. Image was scanned in the Windows Bitmap format. Ventura Publisher (the program used to produce this book) does not import this format, so the clipboard was used to copy the image into Ventura.

© Jerry B. Day 1979

CHAPTER

4

GETTING THE BEST SCAN

Introduction

Your HP ScanJet scanner is capable of producing excellent scanned images. It is used daily all over the world to produce a fantastic variety of documents, including books, magazines, business reports, etc. As with most tools, to produce good results, you must use the tool correctly and effectively. This chapter explains the necessity to calibrate your scanner, how to select originals, and how to use the DeskScan II tools and controls to produce the best scanned image.

Calibrating Your HP ScanJet

The first step in getting the best possible scanned image is to calibrate your HP ScanJet. Calibration is a process that informs the HP DeskScan II software what type of application and printer you will be using to output your scanned images. Most scanned images are output to some form of printer (images can also be scanned for the computer screen only, as in multimedia presentations). Printers have individual characteristics that must be taken into account when scanning. Software applications also have characteristics that your scanner must know about. Software can make changes to scanned images during the printing process. Halftoning of grayscale images is accomplished by software included with the computer's operating system (either PostScript or HP's Printer Command Language, PCL). Printing images for mass distribution using offset or other printing press methods can change the way your scanned image appears. The scanning process begins with the scanner and ends with a printed image. Any step in the process (scanning, software application, printing software, desktop printer, commercial printing process) introduces variables that must be accounted for. The HP DeskScan II calibration method is called *Print Path Calibration.*

Image scanned with incorrect print path calibration.

© 1980 Jerry B. Day

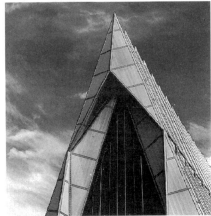

Image scanned with the correct print path calibration.

Accounting for Dot Gain

The most critical variable in the printing process is *dot gain*. Dot gain is a printing defect that causes dots to print larger than they should.

Your scanned image consists of thousands of black dots of the same size. The impression of shades of gray is produced by grouping the same size dots to produce larger dots. The pattern of larger and smaller dots produces the illusion of gray. If the basic dot size increases (or decreases) during the printing process, your halftoned images become darker (or lighter) and lose sharpness. Dot gain can occur when printing on a laser printer, during the production of imagesetter film, or during the printing process when ink is deposited on the paper. Dot gain can be caused on a laser printer by the intensity level being set too high resulting in too much toner being deposited on the paper. It can also be caused by the paper used in the laser printer.

See Also

Refer to chapter 8, "Selecting Printer Paper," on page 172.

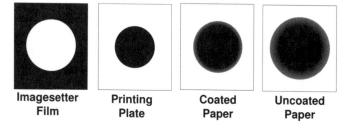

| Imagesetter Film | Printing Plate | Coated Paper | Uncoated Paper |

Illustration of how halftone dots may decrease in size when a printing plate is produced and increase in size when printed on uncoated paper.

Dot gain in the imagesetter film can be caused by incorrect calibration or operation of the imagesetter. Dot gain during the printing process is typically caused by the use of ink-absorbent paper or incorrect operation of the press. While the latter is not common, use of absorbent paper is. Dot gain occurs to some degree in all of the printing processes. Good commercial printers control their processes and keep dot gain to a minimum. You must account for dot gain by scanning a calibration target that was printed on the same press, with the same ink and paper that will be used for printing your images.

DeskScan II Print Path Calibration Process

Your HP ScanJet uses a process called *print path calibration* to communicate to the DeskScan II software information about the printer and software you will be using to output your scanned images. The process uses a calibration target consisting of 256 levels of gray. This target is printed on the printer used for your final output. The printed target is then scanned on your HP ScanJet and a print path calibration established.

HP DeskScan II Print Path Calibration Target.

The calibration target may be printed directly to your printer or from the software application you use to produce your documents. You should print the calibration target directly on your printer if you want to use the printer's default halftone setting. If you wish to use the halftoning capabilities of your software, you should save the calibration target to a file. The file may be in any format supported by your HP ScanJet, but TIFF or PICT are recommended. Import the file into a blank page in your software application. This page is then printed and scanned to create a print path calibration for that particular software application. If you use several printers and software applications for your scanned images, you should establish a print path for each.

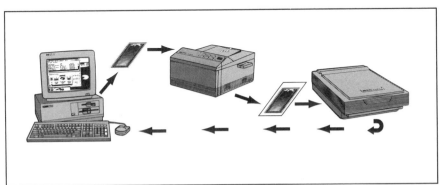

Illustration of a print path calibration from DeskScan II directly to the printer. The printed target is scanned to create a print path calibration.

Print and View Your Images with the Correct Print Path Calibration

If you scan an image using a print path calibration, then print that image to a different printer or load it into a different application (different from the calibration path), the image may not print correctly and may not have a good appearance on your computer screen. For example, if you scanned an image using a print path calibration for an HP LaserJet4 printer, then printed to a different printer, the image will probably not be the way you wanted. Also, if you scan an image using the HP LaserJet4 print path calibration then import the image into an image editor (such as Adobe Photoshop or Aldus PhotoStyler), the image may appear too dark or too light. If you then adjust the scanned image with the image editor to make it appear correct on the screen, it will not look good when printed.

If you plan to import images into an image editor (directly with TWAIN, or indirectly by scanning to a file), you should create a print path calibration for the image editor.

See Also

See page 64 for information on creating a print path calibration for software applications.

> **Tip:**
> You may create as many print path calibrations as you need for each application and for each printer. You may wish to use one of the included print path calibration paths as a starting point for such information as resolution, etc.

Printing a Calibration Target Directly to Your Printer

1. Click on *Print Path* under the *Custom* menu.

2. Click on *New* under Printer Calibration.

3. Click on *Create....*

4. Click on the *Printer* button in the *Send To* box.
   This will send a calibration target directly to the printer you use for your final output (normally this will be your default printer).

Caution

Do not print your calibration targets with a new toner cartridge. New toner cartridges print darker than normal. If you must use a new cartridge, print a number of pages (50 to 100) before printing the target. This allows the toner to stabilize and produce normal print levels.

5. After the target has printed, place it carefully on the scanner bed (the top of the target must be placed next to the document set mark) and slowly close the lid (it must be aligned with the top and right side of the scanner glass).

6. Click on *OK.*

7. Type a name for the calibration path (use the name of your printer; i.e. *LaserJet II* or *LaserJet4).*

Note

When printing a calibration target on the printer you will be using for your final output, be sure to use the same paper you will be using for your final output.

Printing a Calibration Target from Software Applications

1. Click on *Print Path* under the *Custom* menu.

2. Click on *New* under *Printer Calibration*.

3. Click on *Create....*

   Click on the *File* button in the *Send To* dialog box.
   This saves the Calibration Target in a file that you can import into your software applications.

4. Select a file type for the calibration file (use the same file type you will be using for your scanned images). Type a name for your calibration file.

5. Import the calibration target file into the software application that you plan to use to print your scanned images.

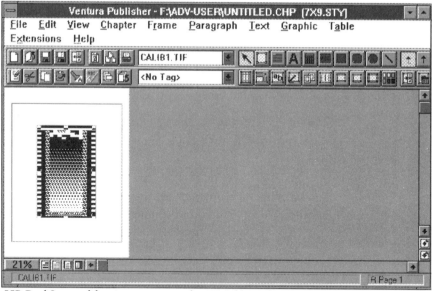

HP DeskScan calibration target saved to EPS file and imported into Ventura Publisher to be printed and scanned to create a print path calibration for Ventura.

Note

When importing the calibration target into desktop publishing and word processing programs that use frames (such as Ventura Publisher, Quark XPress, FrameMaker, etc.) size the frame to 4 inches wide by 6 inches high so that it will print at the correct size for scanning. If your software application has the option of printing crop marks on the page, turn it off before printing the calibration target.

6. Center the calibration target image on the page.

7. Use the software application's print command to print the calibration page using the same printer you will use to print your scanned images.

Caution

Do not print your calibration targets with a new toner cartridge. New toner cartridges print darker than normal. If you must use a new cartridge, print a number of pages (50 to 100) before printing the target. This allows the toner to stabilize and produce normal print levels.

8. After the target has printed, place it carefully on the scanner bed and slowly close the lid (it must be aligned with the top and side of the scanner glass).

9. Click on *OK.*

10. Type a name for the calibration path (use the name of your printer or the software application; i.e. HP LaserJet or PageMaker).

Print Path Calibration for Commercial Printing

If your documents containing scanned images are to be commercially printed using the offset lithographic, letterpress, or other printing method, you must calibrate your HP ScanJet scanner for this process. Printing scanned images with a commercial printing press introduces a number of variables that must be accounted for when scanning the images, including:

- dot gain
- paper stock
- type of ink
- type of printing press.

To calibrate your HP ScanJet scanner for a commercial printing press, the calibration target is imported into your application and printed on film on a high-resolution imagesetter (step 1 in the illustration), the film is used to produce printing plates, and the plates are used to produce a short press run on the commercial press using the same ink and paper that will be used for your projects (step 2). One of the press run pages is scanned to produce your print path calibration for the particular press used (steps 3 and 4).

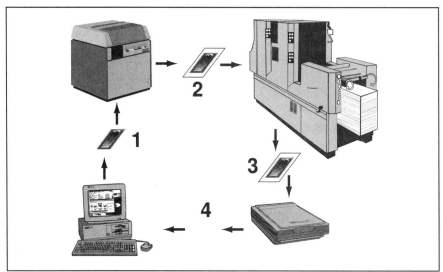

Illustration of the print path calibration process for a commercial printing press.

Producing a Print Path for Commercial Printing

1. Click on *Print Path* under the *Custom* menu.

2. Click on *New* under Printer Calibration.

3. Click on *Create....*

4. Click on the *File* button in the *Send To* dialog box.
   This saves the Calibration Target in a file that you can import into your software applications.

5. Select a file type for the calibration file (use the same file type that you will be using for your scanned images). Type a name for your calibration file.

6. Import the calibration target file into the software application that you plan to use to print your scanned images.

Note

When importing the calibration target into desktop publishing and word processing programs that use frames (such as Ventura Publisher, Quark Express, FrameMaker, etc.), size the frame to 4 inches wide by 6 inches high so that it will print at the correct size for scanning.

7. Center the calibration target image on the page.

Caution

If your software application has the option of printing crop marks on the page, turn off the crop marks before printing the calibration target.

8. Use the software application's print command to print the calibration page to a file on a floppy disk, tape, or removable disk drive.

See Also

Refer to chapter 8, the section "Printing Scanned Images on an Imagesetter."

9. Take the calibration disk file, tape, or removable disk drive to your service bureau or commercial printer.

10. The service bureau or commercial printer produces a plate-ready negative at the resolution you will use for final production.

Tip:
Commercial printing presses are complicated devices. Setting up a press is a skill developed through training and long apprenticeship. Offset lithographic and letterpress printing presses are not designed for limited quantities. Many copies must be run through the press before the correct ink flow and other parameters are established. Be prepared for the expense of producing a limited press run for the purpose of calibration. You can reduce your expense by producing several calibration pages. Most large offset and letterpress printing presses use large plates that contain several pages. You can have them print several calibration targets that you produced at different line screens or with different software applications.

11. Next, the commercial printer produces printing plates, sets up the printing press, and produces a short press run.

12. Ask the commercial printer to print your calibration target on different paper stocks (coated or uncoated, gloss or matte finish, etc.). The printer should not object or charge more as long as the same plates are attached to the printing press.
Mark on the rear of the printed calibration targets information about the paper stock, resolution, etc. and save the targets for future projects.

13. When you have received the printed calibration target from the service bureau or printer, place it carefully on the scanner bed and slowly close the lid (it must be aligned with the top and right side of the scanner glass).

14. Click on *OK.*

15. Type a name for the calibration path (use the name of your printer or the software application; i.e. Lino 330 or PageMaker, etc.).

Beginning with a Good Original

To obtain the best scanned image, you should begin with the best possible original!

Properties of a Good Photograph

- Select photographs that have normal contrast (an even distribution of gray). The most important parts of the photograph should be in the middle range of grays. Avoid high-contrast photographs if possible.

- Avoid photographs that are out of focus or unsharp!
  The HP DeskScan software can sharpen images, but you will get the best results if your original is a sharply focused image. Examine the photo with a magnifying glass or loupe (available at camera stores and art supply houses) to determine if the photo is fuzzy or focused enough for your requirements. If the image is fuzzy, but you still need to use it, scaling it to a smaller size may help. Your HP DeskScan II software has several options for sharpening fuzzy images. Sometimes, portions of an image will be in focus and other parts will be fuzzy. This is usually caused by the photographer shooting the picture with a large aperture opening. The photographic term is *depth-of-field*. You may be able to sharpen the fuzzy portion of the image with one of the image editing or retouching programs.

- Select photographs that do not have scratches, cracks, or other physical damage.
  While retouching and image editing programs can be used to correct some of these defects, retouching a photograph can be time consuming.

  See Also

  Refer to page 90 for more information on HP DeskScan II's sharpening option.

- Try to avoid photographs with stains on them.
  If the original photograph has a stain on it such as ink, coffee, etc., a technique used by professional photographers may eliminate the stain from your scanned image. Place a sheet of transparent film or filter material the same color as the stain on top of the original photograph and scan the image through the material. The stain, being the same color as the film or filter, will not show. Transparent film or filter material in various sizes may be purchased at camera stores or art supply shops.

If possible, always select sharp, correctly focused originals. The sharpening tool can compensate for an original that is slightly out-of-focus, but cannot correct an original that is completely out of focus.

© 1978 Jerry B. Day

Photographs that are over exposed or under exposed (in the camera or the dark-room) cannot always be corrected when scanning. The brightness controls can compensate, but you cannot create detail that is not in the original.

© 1980 Jerry B. Day

Definition of Highlights, Middle Tones, and Shadows

Photographs normally have a range of tones ranging from dark (shadows) to middle tones to light (highlights). In order to use the DeskScan II tools and controls to correct, enhance, or exaggerate the dark, middle, and light tones of your images, you should understand what these terms mean and what they look like. The following example illustrates highlights, shadows, and middle tones in a normally exposed original photograph.

Shadows:
the darkest areas—
nearly black or dark
gray

Middletones:
the middle grays—
no blacks or whites

Highlights:
the lightest areas—
nearly white or light
gray

© 1978 Jerry B. Day

Examples of Photographs with Incorrect Contrast and Exposure

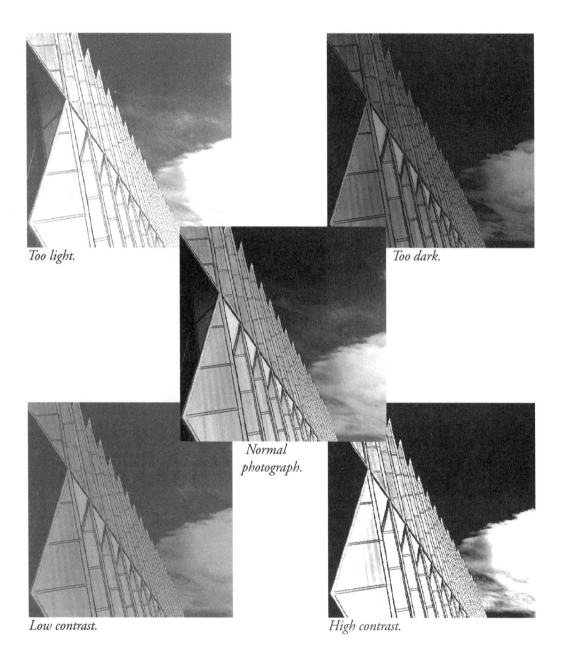

Too light.

Too dark.

Normal photograph.

Low contrast.

High contrast.

Properties of Good Line Art

Some of the same precautions that applied to photographs also apply to line art. Line art can be drawings, sketches, blueprints, or CAD illustrations (computer-aided-design).

- Select line art that is not physically damaged if possible.

  Cracks in the paper, stains, etc. can be difficult and time consuming to remove. If you must scan a damaged image, image editing programs can be used to enhance the image. Tracing the image and converting it to vector format can sometimes eliminate physical damage.

- Avoid line art that is faded or stained.

  If the art is stained and you must have the image, try placing transparent film or filter material the same color as the stain over the art work and scan through it (see page 70 for an explanation of this technique).

See Also

See chapter 6, "Tracing."

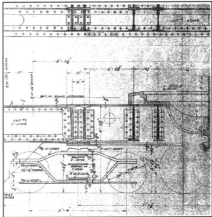

Example of line art damaged by stains. The stain cannot be filtered out (using the technique explained above) because the stain is the same color as the lines in the drawing.

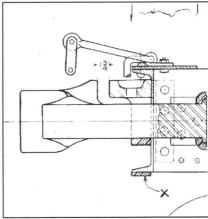

Example of good line art. This drawing had no physical defects. Extraneous pencil marks may be deleted with an image editor.

Tips for Scanning Line Art

- Scan at the resolution of the printer. Line art is not halftoned, so you don't have to be concerned about dots being grouped into halftone cells. If you scan line art at a low resolution, the lines may appear jagged. If you plan to manipulate the scanned line art with a paint program or image editor, you will find it much easier to work with a larger number of dots. If you plan to convert the image from raster (bitmap) to vector format with a tracing program, you will get a better trace from a higher-resolution bitmap.

- Scan at a lower brightness setting. Sometimes line art is not a pure black and white. The image may have faded or may not have been correctly created or printed. Adjusting the brightness level (making the scan darker) may give you a cleaner, sharper image. Line art with very thin lines usually scans better if you lower the brightness level.

- Place acetate over the original line art. Or spray the original with a glossy spray. These two techniques are employed by photographers and graphic artists when reproducing line art. The acetate helps to thicken the lines by diffusing the image and making the scanner think the lines are thicker. Spraying the original with a gloss artist's spray will increase the contrast and make the black areas darker.

Caution

Use artist's spray only on originals that you personally own and that can be replaced. Some originals may be adversely affected by spray. To be sure, test the spray on a sample of the same paper or material as the original.

Getting the Best Scan with the DeskScan II Controls and Tools

If you are scanning a good original photograph or line art, the automatic exposure feature, which sets the brightness and contrast, will probably produce the best possible scan of your original. The automatic exposure feature was designed to measure the highlights and shadows and determine the appropriate settings. If you begin with good originals, this feature will take care of most of your scanning needs.

If your originals are not perfect—are too dark or too light, have too much or too little contrast, you will need to use the DeskScan II tools to correct and enhance your scans. The DeskScan II software includes two sets of tools for controlling the brightness and contrast of your scanned images:

- Highlight and Shadow tool
  Independently adjusts the lightest and darkest portions of your image.

- Emphasis tool
  Adjusts the middle tones separately from the highlights and shadows.

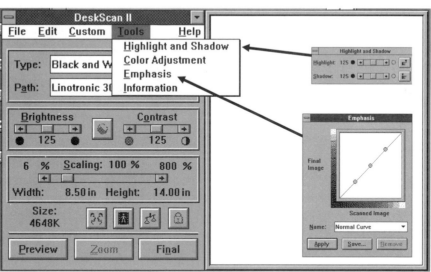

Illustration of the DeskScan II controls and tools.

Scanning Photographs that Are Too Dark or Too Light

Your HP DeskScan II software will automatically set the brightness level to compensate for light or dark originals. With most originals, it will produce an acceptable scan with no action required on your part. If the original was over exposed or under exposed (in the camera or in the darkroom) you can use the brightness control to manually adjust the scanned image. The Highlight and Shadow or Emphasis tools may also be used to compensate for an improperly exposed original. In some cases, the original may have so much contrast, or may be so improperly exposed that the DeskScan tools cannot completely compensate. It is sometimes possible to have a photo lab reprint the original photograph. The photo lab can lighten or darken the print and increase or decrease the contrast.

Normally exposed original photograph scanned with auto exposure at 200 dpi and saved as a 256-level grayscale EPS file.

Dark original photograph scanned with auto exposure at 200 dpi and saved as a 256-level grayscale EPS file.

Sizing and Scaling Images

To produce the best results, your images should be sized and scaled when they are scanned to the size they will be when printed or placed in applications. Resizing images after they have been scanned can produce unacceptable results such as "jaggies." Scanning images at the size they will be used also saves disk space.

See Also

Refer to "Tips for Importing Scanned Images" on page 107.

If you have the Automatic Find feature turned on, DeskScan II will find your image and draw a selection box. You may wish to modify the selection box, by making it larger or smaller. You may wish to change the rectangular selection box to an irregular box by using the Lasso feature. This feature lets you draw a selection box around selected areas of the previewed image. This saves time later when you do not have to delete unwanted areas with an image editor.

When the selection box is set to your satisfaction, you may use the DeskScan II scaling features to enlarge or reduce the image to the size you select. You have two scaling options with DeskScan:

- Uniform Scaling maintains the width and height proportions of the image.
- Non-Uniform Scaling allows you to change the width or height independently. With Non-Uniform scaling you can stretch or shrink an image.

You should use Uniform Scaling to create a normal appearance in your images. With Uniform scaling, when you change the width of the image, you change the height proportionally. Non-Uniform Scaling can be used to distort an image to create a special effect.

Scaling and Resolution

The scaling range of your HP ScanJet scanner and the DeskScan software is determined by the resolution of the image. Scaling and resolution are inversely related: as the resolution increases, the scaling range decreases. The scaling range of the various models of HP ScanJet scanners varies with each model. Consult the user documentation to determine the scaling range at various resolutions.

Examples of Uniform and Non-Uniform Scaling

Image scanned with Uniform Scaling to a size of 2.25 x 2.25 inches.
© 1979 Jerry B. Day

Image scanned with Non-Uniform Scaling. The height is the same as the first image (2.25 inches). The width was changed to 1.60 inches.

Image scanned with Non-Uniform Scaling. The width is the same as the first image (2.25 inches). The height was changed to 1.25 inches.

To Use the Scaling Controls:

To Use Uniform Scaling:

1. If you see two sliding scaling bars, this means Non-Uniform Scaling is active. Click on the *Scale* button to switch to Uniform Scaling.

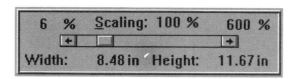

2. To change the width and height of the image simultaneously, slide the slider bar to the right to enlarge the image and slide it to the left to reduce the image.

To Use Non-Uniform Scaling:

1. If you see one scaling bar, this means Uniform Scaling is active. Click on the *Scale* button to switch to Non-Uniform Scaling.

2. To change the width of the image, slide the left slider bar.

3. To change the height of the image, slide the right slider bar.

Using the Automatic Exposure Control

HP DeskScan II's Automatic Exposure Control works like the automatic exposure camera you probably use to shoot your personal or business photographs. Most automatic exposure cameras measure the light reflecting from the scene you are photographing. They determine the darkest and lightest portions of the scene and set the camera's aperture and shutter speed to give you an exposure that is a compromise between the lightest and darkest areas. Automatic exposure works for most situations—but not all. Sometimes the most important area in a scene is either in the dark or light areas. Automatic exposure always attempts to produce an average of the dark and light areas. In those cases, knowledgeable photographers override the automatic control by using the manual exposure control to expose for a particular part of the scene.

The DeskScan II software measures the selected part of the image you are scanning to determine the darkest and lightest portions. It then determines the appropriate brightness and contrast settings to produce an average of the dark and light areas. When you do a Preview scan (if you have the Automatic Find option turned on), DeskScan II will determine the type of image you are scanning, automatically find the edges of the image, and perform an automatic exposure of the selected area. If you change the selection area, click on the Automatic Exposure button so DeskScan II will change the brightness and contrast setting to match the new selection area.

In most cases, if you have a correctly exposed and processed original photograph, the Automatic Exposure control will give you a correct scan of the selected area. Sometimes, a photograph will have very dark or very light areas and the automatic exposure control, attempting to average the dark and light areas, will make the overall image too dark or too light. In this case, you will need to resort to a technique used by photographers. When photographing a scene with very dark or light areas, they know the auto exposure on their cameras will not correctly expose for the dark or light area because it is measuring the entire scene. They will move up to a dark or light area and aim their camera directly at that area. When the camera has automatically set the exposure, they lock the exposure setting and move back to photograph the entire scene. In effect, they are using the camera as a *spot meter* (a hand-held light meter with a narrow angle).

You can use the DeskScan II software in a similar fashion. If Automatic Exposure of the entire scene is not giving you satisfactory results, do the following:

1. Use the mouse to drag a new selection area around just the darkest or lightest area.

2. Click on the *Automatic Exposure* button.

3. Use the mouse to drag the selection area around the parts of the scene you wish in your final scan.

4. Click on the *Final* scan button.

Automatic Exposure of entire image.
© 1976 Jerry B. Day

Automatic Exposure of selected area of the image.
© 1976 Jerry B. Day

Adjusting Light and Dark Areas of an Image

It is not possible to expose shadow (dark) and highlight (light) areas of a scene separately in a camera. The exposure meters in most modern automatic and semi-automatic cameras measure the entire scene and set the exposure to an average between the light and dark areas. Sometimes this results in a photograph that has parts that are too dark or too light. Professional photo labs can sometimes compensate for this with techniques known as *dodging* (making an area lighter), or *burning* (making an area darker). Prints made by one-hour mall labs or quick turnaround services in drug or grocery stores typically do not provide this service.

Scanned with no Highlight and Shadow adjustments.

© 1978 Jerry B. Day

Same photograph scanned after adjustments made with Highlight and Shadow controls.

The Highlight and Shadow controls in the HP DeskScan II software provide the capability of adjusting the light and dark areas of an image independently. Professional photographers use a technique that works in a similar fashion to the Highlight and Shadow control. They use a *spot meter* to measure the lightest and darkest areas of a scene. They then set the camera's exposure so that detail will be recorded in the areas most important in the scene.

The shadow areas of this photograph were lightened with the Shadow tool.
© 1972 Jerry B. Day

To Use the Highlight and Shadow Tool:

1. Click on the *Tools* menu, then click on *Highlight and Shadow*. The Highlight and Shadow tool may be placed anywhere on the screen by dragging it with the mouse. To move the tool, place the mouse cursor on the title bar. Click and hold the mouse button, drag the tool to the location you wish, and release the mouse button.

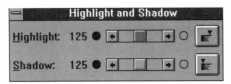

2. Click on the *Highlight* icon.

3. Place the cursor in the lightest (highlight) portion of the image and click the mouse.

4. Click on the *Shadow* icon.

5. Place the cursor in the darkest portion (shadows) of the image and click the mouse. The control will adjust the range of grays between the darkest and lightest.

Note

You can select a point that is not the lightest point or darkest point and force them to be white or dark. This technique is useful if you want to make a portion of the image properly exposed and do not care about the rest. If you use this technique, some areas of the image will be too dark or too light.

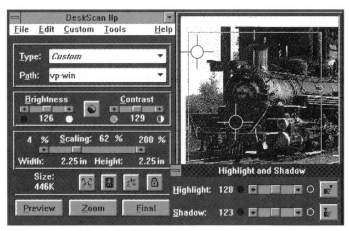

The Highlight and Shadow tool (normally only one cursor appears).

To Manually Adjust the Dark or Light Areas:

In addition to using the Highlight and Shadow control for automatic adjustments, you can use it to independently adjust the shadows or highlights.

To Adjust the Dark Areas:

1. Click on the *Shadow* icon.

2. Place the cursor in the darkest part of the image (or the area you wish to designate as the darkest) and click the mouse. Move the Shadow slider bar to the left to darken the shadow areas or to the right to lighten them.

To Adjust the Light (Highlight) Areas:

1. Click on the *Highlight* icon.

2. Place the cursor in the lightest part of the image (or the area you wish to designate as the lightest) and click the mouse. Move the Highlight slider bar to the left to darken the highlight areas or to the right to lighten them.

Adjusting Middle Tones

The emphasis tool is used to adjust the middle tones of an image separately from the highlights and shadows. In some photographs, you may wish to lighten or darken the middle tones without changing the other areas. Perhaps the center of interest in the photograph is in the middle tones and you wish to enhance it and the shadows and highlights can remain as they are.

The emphasis tool is a curve with three points that may be moved to change the shape of the curve and thereby adjust the density (the darkness or lightness) of the middle tones.

Once you have adjusted the points to your satisfaction, you may save your custom adjustments and use them again. The DeskScan II software comes with several pre-made adjustments that you may use. The adjustments are:

- Normal Curve
- Lighten Middle Tones
- Darken Middle Tones
- Enhance Shadows.

Emphasis Tool Examples

The following examples illustrate the built-in emphasis adjustments.

Image scanned with the Normal Emphasis Curve.

© 1972 Jerry B. Day

middle tone

highlight

shadow

Image scanned with Enhance Shadows Curve applied.

Emphasis Tool Examples Continued...

lighten middle
tone

Image scanned with Lighten Middle Tones Curve applied.

darken
middle tone

Image scanned with Darken Middle Tones Curve applied.

To Use the Emphasis Tool:

1. Click on the *Tools* menu, drag the selection to *Emphasis* and release the mouse button.

   The Emphasis tool may be placed anywhere on the screen by dragging it with the mouse. To move the tool, place the mouse cursor on the title bar. Click and hold the mouse button, drag the tool to the location you wish, and release the mouse button.

2. Place the cursor in the *Name* box, and click and hold down the mouse button.

3. Drag the cursor to the adjustment you wish to use and release the mouse button.

4. Click on the *Apply* button.

   Note

   The Emphasis tool must be open and visible for the adjustments to take effect. If you close the Emphasis tool, the normal adjustment curve is applied to the image.

To develop a Custom Emphasis Curve:

1. Activate the Emphasis tool per step 1 in the previous instructions (the normal emphasis curve will appear in the name box).

2. Use the normal curve or one of the others if one is close to what you wish to use.

3. Place the cursor on one of the three points.

   The lowest point on the curve adjusts the density of the darker middle tones. The high point adjusts the density of the lighter middle tones and the center point adjusts the middle tones.

4. Move the point up to lighten or move the point down to darken.

   The name in the name box changes to *Custom*.

5. When the points are adjusted to your satisfaction, click on *Save....*

6. Type a name for your custom adjustment in the space provided, then click on *Save*.

Enhancing Fuzzy or Unsharp Images

The sharpening control is used to enhance detail in photographs and line art drawings. It does this by increasing the contrast of adjacent pixels. Sharpening can improve the appearance of photographs that suffer from poor focus or unsharpness caused by camera shake. Sharpening does increase image contrast; so you may have to compensate by lowering the contrast of the final scan.

Scanned with no sharpening.   *Scanned with extra heavy sharpening.*

© 1973 Jerry B. Day

Sharpening may reveal defects, such as scratches, spots, lint, dust, etc. in the original photograph or drawing that were not apparent in unsharpened scans. These defects may not be apparent when printing your image on a 300-dpi printer, but may become evident when printing on a 600-dpi printer or high-resolution imagesetter. Also, heavy or extra heavy sharpening may make your image appear grainy. Heavy sharpening of photographs with light areas, such as clouds or a light sky, may create an undesirable effect called an *artifact* in the light area. To eliminate this effect, reduce the amount of sharpening.

Sharpening Line Art

Sharpening may also be used to enhance the detail in line art drawings. Drawings with closely spaced lines or with extremely fine detail will scan better if sharpening is applied. Images that are to be traced should be sharpened. You will want to produce a bitmapped image with the maximum amount of detail for the tracing program to work with. Sharpening increases the contrast of a scanned image and most line art improves with increased contrast.

Line art drawing scanned at 300 dpi with no sharpening.

Line art drawing scanned at 300 dpi with extra heavy sharpening.

Selecting a Halftoning Pattern

The *Samples* option prints six halftone samples of your current previewed image. One sample page of each halftone type is printed. The image is centered and the halftone type is indicated below the image. This option assists you in selecting the best halftone type to use for your image. The image is printed at the size you selected when performing a preview scan of the image. You may print black-and-white samples, color samples, or both. If you choose to print both types, 12 pages of samples will be printed.

After the samples have printed, place them side-by-side and compare the effect created by each halftone type. The differences will be most evident in the highlight (the light) areas of the image. The halftoning pattern is sometimes hard to discern in shadow (dark) areas of the image.

See Also

Refer to chapter 2, "Selecting an Image Type."

Example of Extra Fine halftoning type   *Example of Diffusion halftoning type*

© 1973 Jerry Day

Scanning Halftone Originals

Producing a good scan of an original that has already been halftoned (such as photos from a magazine, book, or newspaper) can be difficult. The halftoned original already has a pattern of dots that can interfere with your HP ScanJet's halftoning pattern. The result may be a moiré pattern that makes the image unacceptable for your purposes.

If you must scan an image that has already been halftoned, there are several things you can do to reduce the moiré pattern:

- Scan the image with the diffusion halftone pattern
  The diffusion halftone pattern will diffuse the image, thereby eliminating the original dot pattern.

Photograph from a magazine scanned as a Fine Halftone.
© 1978 Jerry B. Day

Same magazine original scanned as a Diffusion Halftone.

- Scan the original at an angle. Place the original on the scanner glass at a slight angle.
- Reduce the image when scanning. This will minimize the original dot pattern.

- Use the defocus option in an image editor. Many image editors and photo retouching programs have options that allow you to *soften* or *defocus* the image. You can first soften the image to reduce the dot pattern that results in moirés; you can then apply the program's sharpening tool to resharpen the image without the original dot pattern showing.

- Apply a filter. The various filter patterns available in image editors and such programs as Aldus Gallery Effects can be used to create a special effect and eliminate the moiré patterns.

- Change the screen angle. Many desktop publishing programs give you the option of changing the screen angle of selected images. If yours does not, you can use one of the image editors or photo retouching programs. You can also use a photo separation program. Although these programs are normally used to produce four-color separations for color printing, most allow you to import a monochrome image and change the screen angle. Screen angles are a complex subject. To determine the appropriate angle, consult a commercial printer or be prepared for some experimentation.

Selecting the Appropriate Resolution

One of the most important considerations when scanning images is what resolution to use. Should you scan at the highest possible resolution available? Should you always scan at the same resolution as your printer?

Before answering these questions, it is important to understand that when scanning you have several resolution measurements to consider:

- Scanning Resolution is normally expressed as pixels-per-inch (ppi) or dots-per-inch (dpi). Scanning resolution is set when your scan is made and cannot easily be changed after the scan is made.

- Screen Resolution (computer monitor) is also measured by dots-per-inch, although sometimes the word *pixel* replaces the word *dot* (i.e. pixels-per-inch). A typical MS-DOS/Windows computer screen or monitor has a resolution of from 40 to 95 dpi and a Macintosh a resolution of 72 dpi. This means if you scanned your images at 200, 300, or 400 dpi, you are looking at that image on a lower-resolution screen—you aren't seeing all of the information. This can be critical when scanning line art, you may not know if you are accurately scanning fine lines (in this case, you should use the zoom control to take a closer look at the image). High-resolution monitors are available (at a higher cost of course). If you work with scanned images on a daily basis, you may wish to consider one of these monitors.

- Printing Resolution is also measured in dots-per-inch and can be from 72 dpi to 3,000-dpi depending on the type of printer.

- Lines-per-inch Resolution (also known as screen frequency) determines how large or small the dots will be that are created by the halftoning process. A 300-dpi laser printer will have a lines-per-inch output of approximately 60 lpi, a 600-dpi laser printer will have from 85 to 100 lpi, and a high-resolution imagesetter from 100 to 200 lpi.

Use Print Path Calibrations

In most cases, it is not necessary to scan your images at the highest possible resolution or even to scan at the resolution of your printer. If you are scanning your image as a grayscale or with one of the halftone patterns, the scanning resolution should be appropriate for the linescreen (see Chapter 2 for a discussion of halftoning and linescreens) used by your particular printer. Scanning at a resolution higher than necessary only increases your file size, slows down printing, and in some cases, makes the image impossible to print on a particular printer (if the printer doesn't have enough RAM). Scanning the image as the highest possible resolution or at the resolution of the printer will not necessarily make your image better. The halftoning process uses only as much of the image data as necessary to create the digital linescreen used on that particular printer. If your image has a higher resolution than necessary to create the digital linescreen, the extra data is ignored.

The print path calibrations included with the HP DeskScan II software were calibrated for the best image resolution for that particular device. For example: the print path calibration for an HP LaserJet4 printer is set for an image resolution of 150 pixels-per-inch (or dots-per-inch if you feel more comfortable with dpi). The HP LaserJet 4 has a maximum output of 600 dpi. Why isn't the resolution of the calibration path 600 dpi? The HP LaserJet 4 produces a digital linescreen with a screen frequency of 60 lines-per-inch at a 45-degree angle. The general rule for resolution of scanned images is: scan at approximately twice the linescreen frequency of the printer used for final output. Twice the screen frequency of the LaserJet 4 (60 lpi) is 120; so the print resolution for the LaserJet 4 is 150.

You should not have to calculate scanning resolutions if you use the DeskScan II built-in print path calibrations. If your printer is not included in the built-in calibrations, look at the resolution of one that is similar (use the LaserJet III if you have a 300-dpi printer and the LaserJet 4 if you have a 600-dpi printer).

So What if I Want to Select a Resolution?

The following explanation of scanning resolution is provided for those who wish to know more and for those who do not choose to use the built-in print path calibrations. Selecting a resolution for your scanned images depends upon several factors:

- Are the images line art or photographs?
- What printer will be used for final output?
- Will the images be enlarged or reduced?
- How much disk space will the image require?

Scanning Resolution for Line Art

When scanning line art, you should scan at the resolution of the printer you will be using for your final output, taking into consideration the disk storage limitations of your system and the printer you will be using for final output. As line art is scanned as a one-bit image (refer to Chapter 1 for information on pixel depth), there is no need to be concerned about halftoning.

Scanning line art at the resolution of your printer will help eliminate the jaggies and will provide the best possible bitmap if you plan to trace the image and convert it from a raster (bitmap) image to vector.

Clipart scanned at 100 dots-per-inch.

Same clipart scanned at 300 dots-per-inch.

Scanning Resolution for Grayscale Images

To select the appropriate resolution for scanning and printing grayscale images, you must understand how grayscale images are halftoned and printed on different types of printers. Scanning and printing grayscale images is often a trade-off between levels of gray and detail in the image.

You might ask, why not scan at the resolution of my printer or just go ahead and scan at the highest resolution possible and not worry about it?

And the answer is:

From previous chapters you learned that grayscale images are halftoned with the electronic version of halftone screens. Laser printers and imagesetters produce only one size of dot and they cannot print with shades of gray toner or ink. The impression of continuous tone and shades of gray is created by grouping the same sized dots into different size halftone dots (or cells). The grouping of these dots is determined by the screen frequency (or lines-per-inch), the screen angle, and dot shape. You do not have to be too concerned with screen angle when printing grayscale images. The normal angle is 45 degrees (usually the default with most applications and printers). 45 degrees is used for most black-and-white (including grayscale) because the dots are less apparent in horizontal and vertical lines if the dots are printed on an angle. You should have no problems if you use 45 degrees. You will read or hear much discussion of screen angles. Screen angle becomes critical when producing color separations for four-color printing (because each of the separation plates must have a different screen angle to avoid moiré patterns).

Screen frequency is measured in lines-per-inch or in halftone cells per inch. Typical screen frequencies are 60 lpi for a 300-dpi laser printer, 85 to 100 lpi for a 600-dpi laser printer, and 150 to 300 lpi for high-resolution imagesetters. Screen frequency controls the number of grays and the apparent detail in your images.

It may help in understanding these concepts if you think of the halftone screen as a filter and the screen frequency as how far apart the openings in the filter are.

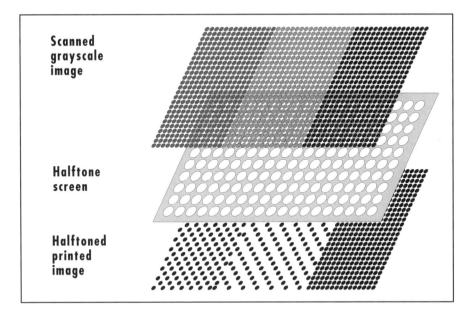

Scanned
grayscale
image

Halftone
screen

Halftoned
printed
image

The halftone screen in conventional halftoning is a real, physical object. The halftone screen in digital halftoning is electronic. It is either in the scanner, in software, or built into the printing device. The halftoning process groups the dots from the original grayscaled bitmap into halftone cells which are groups of black dots arranged to simulate black, white, or shades of gray. Depending on the screen frequency (how many lines in the screen), the halftoning process may use all of the dots from the scanned grayscale image or it may use what it needs and discard the rest. In our filter analogy, if the light passing through the halftone screen were water, some of the water would pass through and some would not.

That is why it is not necessary to scan your images at the highest possible resolution or to scan at the resolution of your printer. The controlling factor is not the resolution of the scanner or the printer, but the halftone screen frequency. This is not to say that resolution is not important or that you can scan at 72 dpi and expect a good image from a 300- or 600-dpi printer. The critical thing to understand is that the resolution of the scanned image must be appropriate for the screen frequency and printer resolution. If the resolution is too high, your files will be larger than necessary. And, if you send files that are larger than necessary to a high-resolution imagesetter, you may pay higher service charges, and in the worst case, the file may not print at all. If your images are halftoned with an incorrect screen frequency (line screen), they may not have enough shades of gray for accurate reproduction—in the worst case, the images would be *posterized* (effect created by limiting the number of shades of gray). When you scan an image as grayscale, screen frequency is controlled by application software (publishing programs, image editors, separation programs, etc.) or by the printer. Choosing the appropriate screen frequency results in a trade-off:

- A fine screen frequency makes you sacrifice the number of available shades of gray.
- A large number of grays requires a coarser screen, thus lowering detail.

When printing to a laser printer, you must choose a resolution that is a balance between detail, shades of gray, and image file size. When printing to a high-resolution imagesetter, the trade-offs are not as limited.

A formula has been developed to measure the relationship between printer resolution, screen frequency, and the number of gray levels produced. The formula is:

(Printer Resolution/Screen Frequency)^2 + 1 = Number of Grays

A typical situation may help to explain this concept:

Image printed at 300 dpi, screen frequency at 60 lpi—how many levels of gray would be produced?

(300/60)^2 + 1 = 26 levels of gray

If we change the printing resolution from 300 to 600 with the same 60 line screen—how many levels of gray?

(600/60)^2 + 1 = 101 levels of gray

This formula indicates that if we leave the screen frequency unchanged, but change the printer resolution, we will increase the levels of gray produced.

What is the Appropriate Resolution for Scanning a Grayscale Image?

So what resolution do you need to scan for laser printers or for high-resolution imagesetters?

You should select a scanning resolution that is two times the halftone screen frequency used by the final output printer. If you use a laser printer for proofing and a high-resolution imagesetter for camera-ready art (CRA), use the screen frequency of the imagesetter, not the laser printer. If you are printing with a 60-line screen, scan at 120 dpi. If you are printing with a 150-line screen, scan at 300 dpi. If you scan at a higher resolution than necessary, the information will not be used by the halftoning process in the software or printer. You will have made files larger than necessary.

There is another formula that will help you determine the appropriate scanning resolution to use:

Screen frequency times two = scanning dpi

For example, if you are using a screen frequency of 85 lpi and you are not enlarging the image, the formula would indicate that you should scan at 170 dpi:

85 lpi x 2 = 170 dpi.

Hewlett-Packard 300-dpi laser printers have a default screen frequency of 60 lpi. With resolution and frequency, 26 levels of gray can be produced. HP 600-dpi PostScript printers have a default screen frequency of 85 lpi producing 50 levels of gray. HP 600-dpi PCL printers have a default screen frequency of 106 lpi producing 33 levels of gray. Remember, increasing the screen frequency (changing the lpi) to a higher number without increasing the resolution of the printer can cause *posterization* (an effect created by limiting the number of shades of gray).

Increasing Perceived Resolution with Interpolation

Throughout this book, I have cautioned against enlarging (or scaling) scanned images. I have recommended scanning the image at the same size it would be in the final document. However, there may be circumstances in which you may have no choice but to enlarge a scanned grayscale image in your software application (example: your grayscale photograph is two inches square and your manager or the editor says it must be four inches square in your document or publication). How can you scan a grayscale photograph, line art drawing, or any image that must be scaled or enlarged later and not have the image become jagged or have an undesirable pattern when printing a halftoned image?

Your HP ScanJet scanner can use a technique called interpolation to increase perceived resolution. Interpolation is a calculation process that creates new pixels between original pixels in the scanned image by dividing the original or existing pixels.

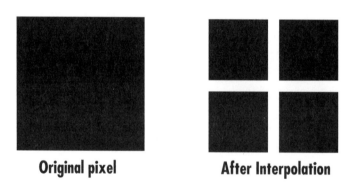

Original pixel   **After Interpolation**

This illustration shows how interpolation creates new pixels by dividing the existing pixels.

Interpolation calculates the range of hues (colors or levels of grays) of the actual pixels and creates new pixels with a smooth gradation between the existing pixels.

Original pixel   **Interpolated pixel**   **Interpolated pixel**   **Original pixel**

This example of the interpolation process being used on a grayscale image shows how new pixels are created between the two originals. The new pixels have gray values that are an average of the two originals.

Interpolation increases the perceived resolution of your HP ScanJet a maximum of two times. For example, an HP ScanJet IIp has an actual optical resolution of 300 pixels-per-inch (or dots-per-inch). Interpolation increases the perceived resolution to 600 pixels-per-inch.

Higher resolutions are particularly welcome when scanning drawings (line art) for direct use in publications or for tracing with one of the drawing or tracing programs. Higher resolution smoothes jagged lines.

Drawing scanned at 400 dpi optical resolution (with no interpolation).

Drawing scanned at 800 dpi (with interpolation).

It is important to remember that interpolation does not actually increase the actual (optical or spatial) resolution of your scanner. Interpolation will not create greater detail in the scanned image. It does permit you to scale or enlarge the image (with some limitations) without the image becoming jagged or without creating patterns when enlarging halftoned images.

CHAPTER

5

USING SCANNED IMAGES
WITH SOFTWARE
APPLICATIONS

Introduction

This chapter explains the process of using scanned images with the many different types of software applications. While it is not possible in this text to explain how to import an image into every application in detail—tips, techniques, and precautions common to most applications will be provided.

Tips for Importing Scanned Images

The following tips and techniques for importing scanned images apply to most types of software applications. For information on specific types of software, continue reading the pages following this section.

- When scanning your image, use the DeskScan II Lasso to crop out any unnecessary white space or white borders. White space creates data and takes up disk space.

- Determine what file formats are supported by your application before scanning the images.

    All of the formats supported by your HP ScanJet are not supported by all software applications.

    Note

    Word processing, desktop publishing, and other software applications use file filters to import graphic images. Some programs automatically install all available file filters during the installation process. Some programs give you the option of installing only selected filters; you select which filters you want during the installation process. If you did not install all of the available filters, you may use the reinstallation process in some programs to install only selected filters. Consult the user documentation for your particular program to determine which formats it supports.

    See Also

    Refer to chapter 3 "Selecting a File Format."

- Some desktop publishing programs have the capability to rotate parts of a page, including text and scanned images. This may slow your printing and screen display. If you wish to rotate a scanned image, import it into an image editor or illustration program, rotate the image, and save it as a new file. Import the new file into your desktop publishing program.

- Scan your image at the exact same size it will be used in the software application.

Tip:
Scanning the image at the same size you plan to use it will save precious disk space, eliminate the need to enlarge or reduce the image in your applications, and will prevent the image from becoming jagged when enlarged. To determine what size to use when scanning an image for inclusion in a word processing document, create the layout and text, then draw a box where the scanned image will be placed. Most word processors and desktop publishing programs have the capability to draw frames or boxes. If your does not, draw a box manually with a pen or pencil. Measure the box and scale the image to that size when scanning. Some word processors now have a frame feature similar to that used by desktop publishing programs. If yours has this capability, you can create a frame and use the frame's measurements when scanning the image.

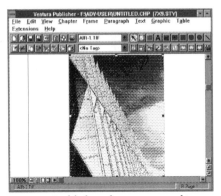

Ventura Publisher places a scanned image inside of a frame. The image assumes the size of the frame. To make the image the same size it was scanned, you must size the frame.

Aldus PageMaker places a scanned image on the page at the same size it was scanned.

- If you must enlarge a scanned image in a software application, use whole number multiples—such as 2 or 4—when you resize the image. For example, if the image is 2 inches wide, and you wish to enlarge it, resize it to 4 inches or 8 inches. Don't make it 2.8 inches or some uneven multiple! This will prevent the image from being distorted.

- Don't enlarge scanned halftoned images (images from newspapers, magazines, etc., that have already been halftoned).

This image was scanned as a 4.67 x 4.50-inch image so that it would fit into a frame of the same size (created in Ventura Publisher) without having to be enlarged or reduced.

© 1978 Jerry B. Day

Word Processors

Word processing software has evolved in the last several years to a point where it is possible to produce many documents with a word processor that would have previously required a high-end desktop publishing program. Multiple-columns, ruling lines, headers, and footers, are just a sampling of the capabilities now available in many word processors. Most word processors for the Macintosh and MS-DOS/Windows systems now have the capability of importing scanned photographs and drawings. Most of these programs permit you to resize scanned images, some allow you to crop parts of the image, and a few give you the capability to place lines or borders around the image.

When importing scanned images into a word processing program, you should determine the final size of the image prior to scanning.

TIFF file imported into Microsoft Word for Windows.

© 1978 Jerry B. Day

Desktop Publishing

While Macintosh and MS-DOS word processors have become increasingly sophisticated and serve the needs of many whose publishing requirements are simple, the production of books or any printed material that requires complex text or image formatting probably demands that you use a desktop publishing program. Programs such as Aldus PageMaker, Ventura Publisher, Quark Xpress, FrameMaker, etc. have the capabilities needed to produce long documents or documents requiring exacting typographic and graphic image standards. These programs differ somewhat in the way they approach page layout and design. Some use the paste-up metaphor in which pages are laid out and pasted up in a similar fashion to manual paste-up with drawing boards and glue. Some programs are highly structured using paragraph tags and frames to control the appearance of text and graphics in the documents. These programs offer powerful image control features including the capability to place complex lines around images, the capability to size and crop images, the capability to change the fill of a picture frame, etc.

Three-line border placed around scanned photograph with the Ventura desktop publishing software used to produce this book.
© 1978 Jerry B. Day

Some desktop publishing programs provide image manipulation features such as contrast control, lightness and darkness control and the capability to control the halftoning method used to print grayscale images. With most publishing programs, the image controls cannot work with Encapsulated PostScript files. It should not be necessary for you to use these controls if you have used the HP DeskScan II software correctly. If you wish to use the image controls in your application programs, you must scan your images as a TIFF, PCX, PICT, or one of the bitmap formats other than PostScript.

Line screen set at 60 lpi with Ventura Publisher.

Line screen set to 85 lpi with Ventura Publisher.

© 1979 Jerry B. Day

Note

While you can use the various controls (contrast, lightness, screen angle, etc.) in your software application, you will probably get better results by using the controls in the DeskScan II software. Use the controls in your application only as a last resort or if the image has been transferred to a location where a HP ScanJet scanner is not available.

Drawing and Illustration Programs

Scanned bitmapped images can be used with drawing and illustration software such as CorelDRAW, Adobe Illustrator, Aldus Freehand, etc. While these programs produce vector graphic files and are primarily designed to work with vector formats such as Encapsulated PostScript, HPGL (Hewlett-Packard Graphics Language), DFX (AutoCAD format), etc., they can import bitmapped files for use as templates for tracing or for use as part of a vector image. Several of these programs have the capability to rotate, stretch, or shear bitmapped images, to create masking effects over bitmapped images, and other special effects. Vector graphic applications such as these cannot directly modify the bitmapped image. They cannot, for example, change the contrast, lighten or darken, or perform any of the other modifications that can be accomplished using image editors or paint programs. If you wish to use a bitmapped image in a vector graphic application, make any modifications to the image in an image editor prior to importing it into the drawing or illustration program.

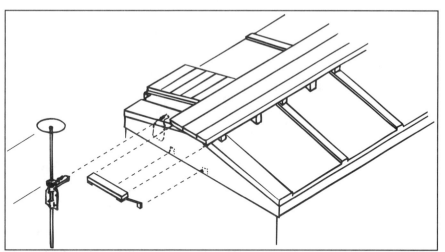

Example of a technical illustration produced by tracing a bitmapped image with Adobe Streamline tracing software then adding detail with Adobe Illustrator drawing program.

© San Juan Car Company

Image Editors

Why would you need an image editing program when the DeskScan II software included with your HP ScanJet scanner includes the capability to lighten or darken images, change the contrast, sharpen images, etc.? The DeskScan software provides the control needed to scan and enhance most images. However, most scanned images require some adjustment or manipulation. The original image may have been incorrectly exposed or printed and require darkening or lightening. The original may have been damaged, or you may wish to significantly modify the image from the original. Image editing programs may be thought of as a photographic darkroom on your computer. With one of these programs, you have the capability of changing the contrast of part of an image, lightening or darkening all or parts of the image, deleting part of an image, sharpening or blurring all or part of the image, etc. You can combine two images into one, create montages, or copy part of the image and paste it onto another part.

Aldus PhotoStyler image editing program being used to delete the background from a scanned grayscale TIFF file.

The image editing software category includes programs ranging from relatively simple paint programs to sophisticated image manipulation and photo retouching programs. Programs such as Adobe Photoshop, Aldus PhotoStyler, ZSoft Photofinish, Ventura PicturePro and others give you the capability to modify and manipulate scanned images. These programs provide powerful image editing and manipulation tools.

Original photograph scanned as a 256-level grayscale file at 200 dpi.

© 1979 Jerry B. Day

Same file after Adobe Photoshop dodging tool is used to lighten parts of the image.

Emboss filter applied with Adobe Photoshop.

© 1979 Jerry B. Day

Find Edges filter applied with Adobe Photoshop.

Original photograph scanned at 200 dpi and saved as 256-level grayscale EPS file.
© 1978 Jerry B. Day

The same photograph after the background was deleted using Adobe Photoshop image editing software.

Computer-Aided Design (CAD)

Computer-aided design (CAD) programs are available for both Apple Macintosh and MS-DOS/Windows systems. Autodesk AutoCAD, Drafix CAD, Generic CADD, are just a few of the programs available. Some programs are available for both systems. CAD programs may be thought of as specialized (2-D or 3-D) drawing programs. CAD programs are used in engineering, manufacturing, and technical environments to design everything from toys to spacecraft. Many engineers and designers use high-end CAD software running on high-end work-stations. As microcomputers have evolved, becoming more powerful and faster, CAD has become available to the Macintosh and MS-DOS user. CAD is typically used to produce engineering drawings from specifications or to design directly in the CAD software.

Many companies have been searching for a way to convert paper drawings to a digital form. Perhaps it is an old drawing that was produced prior to the acquisition of CAD; or it could be a rough sketch drawn on an envelope or napkin in a meeting. A HP ScanJet scanner combined with tracing software provides a solution—a method of getting those paper drawings into the CAD software where they may be modified and enhanced. Several tracing programs are available that can convert a scanned bitmapped image to vector formats recognized by CAD programs.

See Also

Refer to chapter 6 for information on tracing and page 219 for a list of tracing software programs.

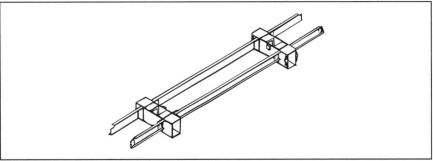

Drawing scanned as TIFF file, traced with Adobe Streamline, saved in SLD (vector format), and imported into AutoDesk AutoCAD.

© San Juan Car Company

Desktop Document Management

Desktop Document Management (DDM) software is a specialized application that allows you to scan, store, retrieve, and manage documents. You can combine DDM software with your HP ScanJet scanner and create an electronic filing and retrieval system. It can be used to replace systems that use film or microfilm to store and retrieve documents. Both text and graphics may be included in the documents that are stored. DDM can be used as archival storage of paper document originals that are destroyed or can be used in place of paper documents (such as in a library where rare and delicate documents cannot be handled by the public).

Most desktop document management applications include a database function that lets you retrieve documents with keyword searches (or other retrieval methods). Many DDM programs include the capability to send and receive documents with fax or e-mail or to route documents to specific individuals on a network.

Most desktop document management software includes optical character recognition (OCR) capabilities. This allows you to scan a document as an image, convert it to text, then search for word or phrases within the document.

See Also

Refer to page 221 for a list of desktop document management software programs.

KeyFile desktop management software.

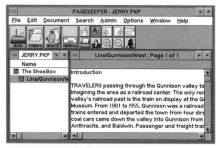

PageKeeper desktop management software.

Incorporating Images Directly into Software Applications with TWAIN

To incorporate images into your documents, it was typically necessary to first exit from your word processor, desktop publishing program, image editor, or other software application. You then had to load the DeskScan II software, scan your image, save it to a file, leave DeskScan II and return to your application to import the scanned image.

Now there is a way of scanning images that eliminates the need to exit from your application. TWAIN is a software interface standard developed by Hewlett-Packard and other hardware and software manufacturers. TWAIN is supported by many image editors, desktop publishing programs, and word processors. Applications that do not currently support TWAIN will probably add support in a future release of their product.

TWAIN allows you to scan directly into the application using HP DeskScan II. All of the features and functionality of DeskScan II are available to you. TWAIN works by establishing a link between your application and DeskScan II.

Photos such as this example can be scanned directly into applications using TWAIN.
© 1977 Jerry B. Day

Example of a TWAIN Scanning Session

The following example illustrates how you can use TWAIN to scan an image directly into an application (in this example: Adobe Photoshop). To use TWAIN, you must be using an application that supports TWAIN.

I. The first step is to establish a link between your application and DeskScan II. You do this by first choosing your application's *File* menu item titled *Acquire.* Next choose *Select Source,* then choose *DeskScan II.*

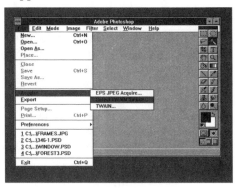

2. Now you can scan an image directly from the application. Choose *Acquire* from the *File* menu in your application. This transfers you to DeskScan II which automatically performs a preview scan.

3. Use the DeskScan II software as you normally would.

4. When you click the DeskScan II *Final* scan button, the image will be scanned and placed in your application.

See Also

Refer to the user documentation for TWAIN applications to determine how each particular application implements TWAIN.

Example of an image scanned directly into Adobe Photoshop using TWAIN. Image was exported from Photoshop as a 256-level grayscale EPS file and imported into this book.

© 1980 Jerry B. Day

CHAPTER
6

TRACING

Introduction

Use this chapter to learn how to convert bitmapped images to vector format using tracing software or drawing software with tracing capabilities.

Raster versus Vector

Raster Graphics

There are two types of graphic files: *raster* and *vector*. Raster files are also referred to as *bitmapped*, or *paint* files. Raster files are produced by paint or image editor software programs and by scanners. The images produced by your HP ScanJet scanner are raster files. Raster images are mathematical descriptions of points on a grid. Each cell in the grid is filled with black or with white.

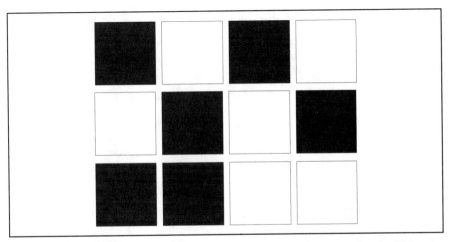

The most widely used term for this type of file is *bitmapped* and will be the term used most often in this book. Bitmapped images can be black-and-white line art, grayscale images, or color. The advantages of bitmapped images are that they can be edited in a paint program or image editor and they are widely used in word processing programs, desktop publishing, presentation programs, etc. The major difficulty with bitmapped images is that they loose their smoothness or sharpness when enlarged and become "jagged."

Bitmap Disadvantages

Bitmapped images have two limitations that you should be aware of:

- The quality of bitmapped images degrades when enlarged within software applications—the image may be unsharp or "jagged."

- Bitmapped images printed on high-resolution imagesetters (such as Linotronic or Agfa) do not increase in resolution. A 300-dpi bitmapped image prints at 300 dpi even on a 2,450-dpi imagesetter.

Photograph scanned as a 256-level grayscale Encapsulated PostScript (EPS) file.

© 1980 Jerry B. Day

The same EPS file enlarged 700 percent.

Vector Graphics

Object-oriented graphics or *vector graphics* are the other form of graphical image. Vector graphic files are also called *draw files*, or *object-oriented files*. Vector files are also mathematical descriptions; but rather than describing each point in the grid, vector graphics use lines, curves, and shapes.

A bitmap description of an object would read something like this: "make cell 1 black, make cell 2 white, make cell 3 white, make cell 4 black, make cell 5 white, etc." A vector description of an object would read: "draw a line from point a to point b and make it one cell wide" (this is a very simplistic description of a more complex process).

Bitmapped files are almost always larger than vector files because bitmaps must describe each cell; whereas, the vector only indicates the beginning point and ending point of a line.

Vector graphics, unlike bitmapped graphics (raster images), are resolution and device independent. *Resolution independence* means vector graphic images can be enlarged without losing any sharpness or without developing the "jaggies."

Device independence means vector graphics may be printed at the highest resolution of the printer you are using. If you use a 300-dpi printer, the vector graphic will print at 300 dpi. If your printer is a 600-dpi device, the vector graphic will print at 600 dpi. You may even print on a high-resolution output device such as an imagesetter at 2,450 dpi, and the vector graphic will print at that resolution.

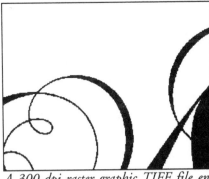 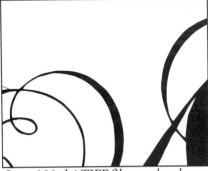

A 300-dpi raster graphic TIFF file enlarged 600 percent.

Same 300-dpi TIFF file traced and saved as a vector graphic file, then enlarged 600 percent.

What is Tracing?

Tracing, also known as *raster-to-vector conversion* is a process of drawing lines around a bitmapped graphic image and saving it in one of the vector formats. Tracing a bitmapped image removes the limitations of the bitmap and produces a higher quality image. A vector graphic file is smaller in disk space than a bitmapped graphic file and will also print faster.

To trace a bitmapped image, you will need a drawing or illustration program with tracing capability (such as Adobe Illustrator, Aldus Freehand, CorelDRAW, etc.) or a dedicated tracing program (such as Adobe Streamline or CorelTRACE). You may need a paint or image editing program to prepare the scanned image for tracing.

Drawing or illustration programs with tracing capability typically offer manual and automatic tracing modes. Manual tracing offers great control over the areas to be traced but requires more time. Automatic tracing offers speed, but less control.

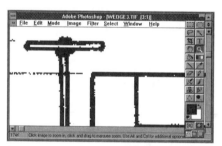

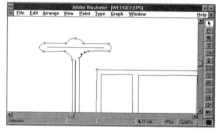

Image scanned as 400-dpi TIFF file and enlarged 400 percent in Adobe Photoshop. Note the individual pixels.

Same image after being traced and saved as a vector graphic and enlarged 400 percent in Adobe Illustrator (image is shown in artwork editing mode—when the image is printed, the outlines are filled with black).

Tracing software usually offers two styles of tracing:

- Outline Tracing. The program traces the outline or perimeter of a line.
- Centerline Tracing. The program traces the center of a line.

You may wish to experiment with the manual and automatic modes and the outline and centerline styles to determine which produces satisfactory traces for you.

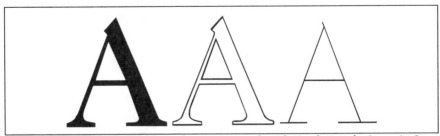

Original character (left). Same character traced with Outline style (center). Same character traced with Centerline style (right).

How to Trace a Bitmapped Image

The following steps illustrate a typical tracing procedure. The procedure will vary according to the particular software programs used.

1. Scan the original image as a black-and-white drawing, cropping the image as closely as possible to minimize file size. Use the contrast and intensity controls to maximize fine details. Scan the image at a high resolution (at least 300-dpi) and sharpen as appropriate to give the tracing program the best image possible.

2. If necessary, import the scanned image into a paint program or image editor. You may wish to delete parts of the image or modify it prior to tracing.

3. Import the scanned image into a tracing, drawing, or illustration program.

4. Trace the scanned image manually or automatically and save the traced image in one of the vector formats (usually Encapsulated PostScript, Computer Graphics Metafile (CGM), PICT, etc.).

5. If necessary, modify or edit the traced image in the drawing or illustration program.

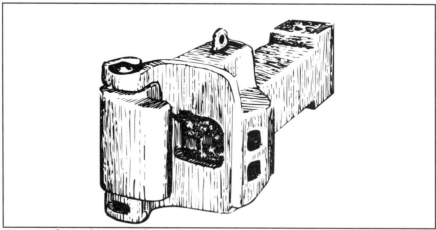

Drawing from a historic industrial equipment catalog (1916). Scanned as black-and-white drawing, traced with Adobe Streamline, and modified with Adobe Illustrator.

Tracing Blueprints

Blueprints have been used in industry for years. Blueprints are copies made from original engineering or manufacturing drawings. Manufacturing, engineering, architectural, and many other technical organizations utilize blueprints in their production or design processes. Many blueprints were created prior to the introduction of computer-aided drafting (CAD) systems. Organizations often find it necessary to update historic or out-of-date blueprints. They want to be able to update measurements or make changes to the shape of the object itself.

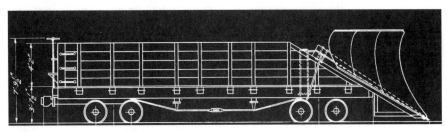

A historic blueprint scanned as a TIFF file at 300-dpi.

An HP ScanJet scanner and tracing software provides the capability of scanning a blueprint and converting it to the vector format utilized by CAD systems. Scanning a blueprint as a bitmapped image may not be satisfactory due to the difficulty of editing detailed illustrations in paint-type programs.

To scan a blueprint for tracing, scan at the maximum dpi possible, use the negative feature in the DeskScan II software to reverse the image, and use maximum sharpening. You will want to ensure the best possible bitmap for the tracing program to work with.

After scanning the blueprint, you may wish to edit the image with a paint program or image editor to delete any dimensions or text that you will not wish to be in the traced image. You may also wish to delete lines or portions of the drawing not needed in your tracing.

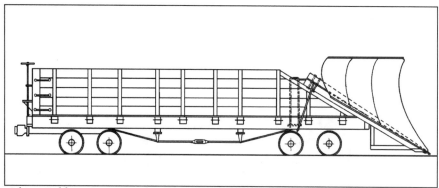

A historic blueprint reversed and scanned as a 300-dpi TIFF file. Text and dimension lines deleted with Adobe Photoshop.

After the bitmapped image has been edited in your paint program or image editor, you can trace the image with a tracing program or with the built-in tracing capabilities of your drawing program.

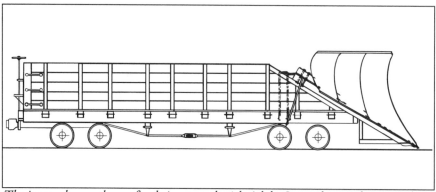

The image shown above after being traced with Adobe Streamline and imported into Adobe Illustrator.

The advantages of tracing a bitmapped image so that it is converted to a vector format include:

- The traced image can be imported into an illustration or drawing program (such as Adobe Illustrator or CorelDRAW) or into a CAD program (such as AutoCad) where it can be modified.
- The traced image in vector format will not suffer from "jaggies" when enlarged.

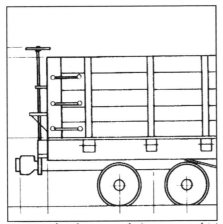 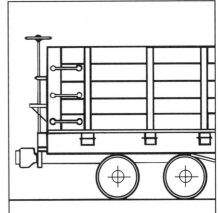

A 300-dpi bitmapped (raster graphic) TIFF file enlarged 200 percent.

A 300-dpi TIFF file traced and converted to PostScript (EPS) vector graphic file and enlarged 200 percent.

Tracing Photographs

One seemingly obvious use of the tracing procedure would be to trace a grayscale or color photograph and convert it to a vector line art image. Photographs often are too detailed for use in technical documentation. One of the advantages of line art is that only selected details are shown and emphasis may be directed to a particular area or part.

Can photographs be traced and converted to line art? The answer is yes: but the process requires some effort! When tracing a scanned photograph, often there is so much detail and information in the scanned image, the tracing program produces an image so complex that it will not print (the complexity of the image exceeds the memory limitations of the printer). The image also may be difficult if not impossible to edit with a drawing or illustration program (complex images can exceed the memory limitations of the computer system and either load extremely slowly or not load at all). The image may be so complex it cannot be imported into word processing or desktop publishing programs. Tracing software is designed to search for the edges of lines or segments and a scanned grayscale image often does not contain a well-defined edge. It may be possible to scan a grayscale photo as line art and then trace it. If the photo has a pure white or black background in which the edges of the subject matter are well-defined, it is possible to obtain a good trace. A usable tracing can sometimes be produced by scanning the photograph as a 16-level grayscale image and using the tracing software to produce a posterization effect by reducing the number of gray levels to eight or four.

Sometimes the only solution is to manually trace the photograph using a graphic arts or photo light table and conventional tracing paper. The tracing is then scanned and retraced using tracing software or the built-in tracing capability of drawing or illustration software. This may seem like a lot of effort, but this may be the only way to produce a line art tracing of the photograph—the results from this method can be dramatic.

Image scanned as 16-level grayscale photograph with maximum sharpening. Brightness and contrast levels increased slightly to produce a pure white background. Image saved as a TIFF Compressed file.

© San Juan Car

Line art image produced by tracing the TIFF file shown above with Adobe Streamline. The posterization effect was produced by setting number of colors to four in Streamline.

CHAPTER

7

SCANNING TIPS AND TECHNIQUES

Introduction

This chapter is a collection of tips, tricks, and techniques for using your HP ScanJet scanner more effectively and creatively.

Scanning Photographic Proof Sheets

A technique often used by professional photographers and graphic designers can be useful to you when producing a document that includes photographs. Prior to enlarging their negatives, photographers and designers often will produce a proof sheet (also called a contact sheet). A proof or contact sheet is a photograph of all the negatives from one roll of 35 mm or 120 film (120 film can produce negatives that are 6 cm x 6 cm, 6 cm x 4.5 cm, or 6 cm x 7 cm). Proof sheets are usually made on one sheet of eight by ten inch photographic paper by placing the paper in contact with the negatives and exposing the paper. Eight by ten inch paper normally allows 36 exposures of 35 mm film or 12 exposures of 120 film to be placed on one page.

The proof sheets are the same size as the negatives, so they should not be used for final output. Photographers and designers use proof sheets to select pictures for enlargement and to indicate to the photo lab which parts of the photograph to darken or lighten.

© 1992 Jerry B. Day

You can do even more with a proof sheet and your ScanJet scanner. You can scan selected pictures from the proof sheet, sharpen and scale them to a larger size, and use them in your document temporarily until the photo lab has produced your enlargements (designers call this *for-position-only* or FPO). When you receive the enlargements from the photo lab, scan them to replace the FPO scans. With some DTP or word processing programs, if you use the same file name that you used for the FPO scans; the new scans will automatically replace the first scans in your document.

You may wish to give the photo lab a sample of your document with the for-position-only (FPO) scanned images in place. The photo lab will be able to see how you will use the enlarged pictures in the publication. They can then produce a photographic print appropriate for scanning and reproduction.

Darken this area

You may also wish to annotate the printed sample, showing any areas you wish darkened or lightened, and which parts of the picture you want included or omitted (photo labs and some image editors call this *cropping*). You can annotate the sample with your publishing or word processing software, or you may wish to mark on the sample with a marker or pen as shown. If you annotate with your publishing or word processing software, be sure to delete these annotations in your final document.

Scanning Black-and-White Negatives

If you have an HP ScanJet IIcx scanner with the optional transparency adapter, you can scan black-and-white negatives directly to produce FPO images. You can also scan black and white negatives to produce proof sheets (or contact sheets). Black-and-white photographic proof sheets typically cost from four to eight dollars each, but a proof sheet scanned and printed on a laser printer will cost approximately ten cents. Proof sheets printed on 300- or 600-dpi laser printers will not be acceptable for most professional photographers or for publishing purposes. These proofs will not have the resolution of a proof sheet made on photographic paper. You cannot examine fine detail in a laser proof with a magnifying glass or photographer's loupe. Proof sheets produced with the transparency adapter and printed on a laser printer may exhibit some posterization effects and should not be used to judge correct contrast in the negatives. But scanned proofs printed on a laser printer may be acceptable for determining which pictures are out-of-focus or composed incorrectly, etc. and which ones are good enough to be enlarged.

Scanning a negative for-position-only provides the same advantages (and limitations) as scanning a photographic proof sheet. The images you obtain using this method will, in most cases, not be acceptable for final output. You should use this method to produce FPO scanned images for use in planning publications. You should have a good-quality photographic print made as soon as possible and use it for scanning the final image.

Emergency conditions, such as this accident and fire, may dictate that you immediately produce a scanned (FPO) image for planning a publication. Using the transparency adapter to scan a negative provides the fastest method to do this.

© 1985 Jerry B. Day

To Scan Photographic Negatives

1. Insert the negatives into the transparency guides so that they are positioned in the optimal location. Place the guides on the scanner glass emulsion side (the dull side) up (you can include all of the negatives from a 36-exposure roll of 35mm film, four 4x5-inch negatives, or one 8x10-inch negative).

2. Scan the negatives at 100 percent scaling.

3. Convert the negative image to a positive with the Reverse Control.

4. Scan with the Sharpening Control set to *extra heavy*.

Caution

When you have finished scanning your negatives, you should protect them from scratches and other possible damage by placing them in protective sleeves. Photo supply stores sell archival-quality clear preserver sleeves that will protect your valuable film from physical and environmental damage. Proof prints and scans can be made directly through these sleeves.

Note

Reversing the negative image and using the Sharpening Control will increase the contrast of the scanned image. Use the Emphasis Control to reduce the contrast to a normal level.

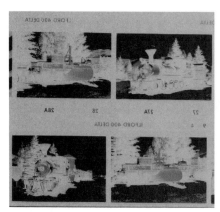

Example of a scanned negative.
© 1991 Jerry B. day

Image converted from negative to positive with the Reverse Control.

Using Macros to Scan Automatically

Macro recorders are software utility applications that permit you to record a series of keystrokes and/or mouse clicks and replay the recorded combination to automate frequently performed tasks. A macro recorder utility (Windows Macro Recorder) is included with Microsoft Windows. Third-party utilities such as Norton Desktop, ProKey, and Hewlett-Packard NewWave are available for Windows that provide greater capabilities than the Windows Macro Recorder.

Note:

The macro recorder and scripting software included with Apple System 7 Pro (AppleScript) does not work with DeskScan II on the Macintosh. Third party macro software may work with DeskScan II on the Mac, but I have not had the opportunity to test these options.

You can use the macro recorders to record while you scan a photograph or drawing; you may then play back the macro to automatically scan other photographs or drawings of the same size. If you have a large number of photos or drawings of the same size, a macro can be a great time saver. With a macro, someone who does not know how to use the DeskScan software can automatically scan photos and drawings by placing the originals on the scanner and playing back the macro.

To Record a Macro with Microsoft Windows:

1. Start the Windows Recorder application (Recorder is installed in the Accessories group by the Windows startup program).

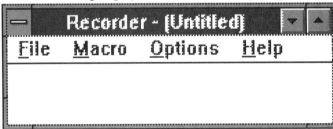

2. Start the DeskScan Software.

3. Reduce the Program Manager to an icon so that only DeskScan and the Recorder programs are shown on the screen.

4. Size the Recorder window so that it will fit in the space below the DeskScan window.

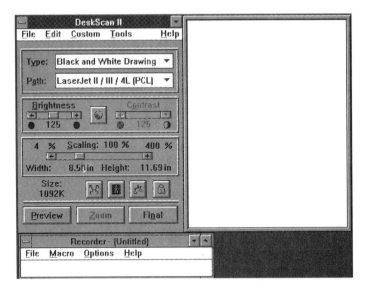

5. From the Macro menu, choose *Record.* The Record Macro dialog box will appear.

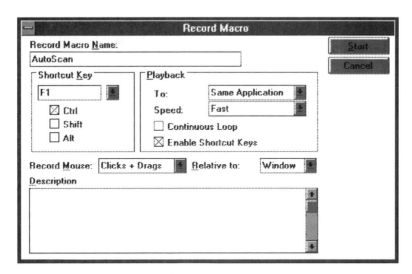

6. In the *Record Macro Name* box, type a name for the macro. The macro name may be up to 40 characters.

7. Select a shortcut key combination to start the macro. (you do not have to select a shortcut combination to record a macro, but it will be easier to start your macro if you do). The key combination may be any combination of Ctrl, Shift, and Alt plus one key selected from the drop-down list.

8. Leave *Playback* set to *Same Application.*

9. Set Speed to *Recorded Speed* if you wish the macro to play back at the same speed as you performed the scan. If you wish the macro to play back as fast as possible, set the Playback speed to *Fast.*

10. Click on *Start.*

11. Perform your scan, selecting the options and preferences you wish to use on similar images.

12. To stop the Macro Recorder, press the Ctrl key and the Break key simultaneously.

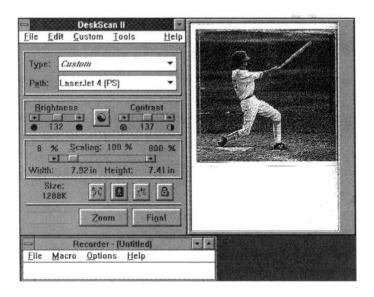

13. Click on *Save Macro*, then click on *OK*. Your macro is complete.

To Play Back the Windows Macro

After you have recorded the macro, you may use it to automatically scan materials that are the same size. If you assigned a shortcut key combination, you may play back the macro by pressing the selected keys. You must have the Macro Recorder active.

1. Start the Macro Recorder application. Select the macro you created to scan images from the list shown.

2. From the Macro menu, click on *Run*, or double-click the macro name.

To Stop the Windows Macro While It Is Running.

1. Press the *Ctrl + Break* keys.

2. When the dialog box appears, confirming the cancellation, click on *OK.*

See Also

Refer to the Microsoft® Windows™ *User's Guide* for more information on recording and playing macros.

You can scan photographs or line art of the same size and same type automatically with a macro.

© 1979 Jerry B. Day

Scanning Clip Art

Newspaper editors, newsletter publishers, graphic artists, and others involved in publishing for many years have used graphic illustrations produced by clip art publishing companies. *Clip art* is so named because the illustrations were "clipped" from the clip art books and pasted in the publications. The clip art business is an old established part of the publishing profession. Several of the clip art publishing companies have been in business for over one hundred and fifty years.

Scanned as a 16-level grayscale and saved as a TIFF file.

Today, many desktop publishers, who do not have access to professional artists, use electronic clip art to enhance their documents. Electronic clip art is available from new clip art studios specializing in computer clip art and from the traditional clip art publishers who have expanded into the computer clip art business. The variety and quality of much of the computer clip art is extremely high and will serve your purposes in many cases.

However, there is more clip art available in the traditional printed form and the cost of the printed clip art is much less than ready-to-use computer clip art. The price of an average book of clip art is about five or six dollars, and these books contain hundreds of illustrations in many sizes and styles. Most of the clip art is not copyrighted (some is, so be sure to check before you use it). Some of the clip art publishers have restrictions as to how many illustrations you may use per project (usually ten maximum).

The variety of subject matter seems endless. Many of the clip art publishers have been in business many years and offer material from many time periods, not always modern (as seems to be the case with computer clip art). You can find Victorian, Art Nouveau, Deco, etc. You will find entire books of borders, graphic symbols, backgrounds and patterns; the list could go on for pages. A sampling of titles from one publisher includes: *Medical and Health Services,* *Travel and Tourist, School and Educational, Nautical and Seashore, Baby and Infant Care, Sports, Performing Arts, Weddings, House and Real Estate.*

Combine several of these clip art collections with your HP ScanJet scanner and you have an unlimited source of graphics for your company newsletter, proposal, report, book, or any other document that requires visual communication.

Scanning a clip art image offers several advantages for the desktop publisher:

- You do not have to clip the illustrations from the book (they can be used again and again).
- You don't have to physically paste them in place with glue or tape.
- You may edit or modify the illustrations to better suit your needs.
- You may trace the images and convert them to vector format so they may be enlarged without becoming "jagged."

Line art or Grayscale?

Most clip art images should be scanned as line art as they contain only black and white. Some clip art images scan better as a black-and-white gray scale photograph. An increase in contrast may be necessary when scanning as grayscale.

Clip art scanned as line art.

Clip art scanned as black-and-white photograph.

Modifying Clip Art

Scanning clip art gives you many options for modifying the clip art images to suit your needs and requirements. You can make changes when scanning, such as changing the contrast to create a special effect or converting the image to a negative.

Image scanned as a TIFF file.
© Volk Clip Art

Image reversed and scanned as a 300-dpi TIFF file.

Clip art image scanned as line art with normal brightness and normal contrast.

Same clip art image scanned as line art with brightness set to maximum and contrast set to minimum.

Text may be added to your scanned image with a paint program, image editor, or illustration software.

Caution

Text added to a scanned image with a paint program or image editor becomes part of the image. The text cannot edited as text, it must be edited pixel by pixel. Some drawing programs permit you to add text to a scanned image on a separate layer that can be edited as text.

Text added to a traced clip art file with Adobe Illustrator. Text added to a vector graphic can continue to be edited as text. Text added directly to a bitmapped image cannot.

Text added to a TIFF file with Adobe Illustrator drawing program. Text is on a separate layer from the image. Text may be edited independently of the bitmapped image.

You may also make changes directly to the bit mapped image with an image editor or special effects software such as Aldus Gallery Effects, Adobe Photoshop, Aldus PhotoStyler, etc.

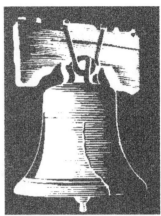

Graphic pen effect applied to TIFF file with Aldus Gallery Effects.

Film grain effect applied to TIFF file with Aldus Gallery Effects.

Emboss filter applied to file with Adobe Photoshop.

Wind filter applied to file with Adobe Photoshop.

Tracing Clip Art

If you plan to enlarge your scanned clip art or you want to print on a high-resolution laser printer (such as the HP LaserJet 4) or imagesetter, you may wish to trace the bit mapped clip art with the tracing feature in your drawing program or a dedicated tracing program (such as Adobe Streamline). Tracing the bitmapped image will eliminate the "jaggies" that result when you greatly enlarge a bit mapped image. The traced image becomes a vector graphic file that you can manipulate in a drawing program. The traced image will print at the highest resolution of the printer, whereas the bitmapped image will always be the resolution it was scanned.

See Also

Refer to Chapter 6 for information on tracing.

Image scanned as a 300-dpi TIFF file, traced with Adobe Streamline, and converted to PostScript EPS.

Image reversed and scanned as a 300-dpi TIFF file, traced with Adobe Streamline, and converted to EPS.

beautiful effect can be created by tracing one of the ornamental capital characters from a clip art book and using it as the first letter in a paragraph as in this example (graphic artists and designers call these "drop caps").

The traced image may be modified in your drawing or illustration software.

Image scanned as a 300-dpi, TIFF file, traced with Adobe Streamline and converted to PostScript (EPS), image fill changed from 100 percent black to 40 percent black with Adobe Illustrator.

Image reversed and scanned as a 300-dpi TIFF file, traced with Adobe Streamline and converted to PostScript (EPS), image fill changed from 100 percent black to 40 percent black with Adobe Illustrator.

Clip art Image scanned as a 300-dpi TIFF file, traced with Adobe Streamline, and saved as a PostScript (EPS) file.

Same EPS graphic with image fill changed in Adobe Illustrator.

Combining Bitmapped and Vector Images

Traced vector images may be combined with bitmapped images to create special effects. In the following example, the picture frame clip art was scanned as a TIFF file. It was then traced with Adobe Streamline and saved as a PostScript vector file. The photograph was scanned as a grayscale image and placed on top of the frame image to produce the effect shown below.

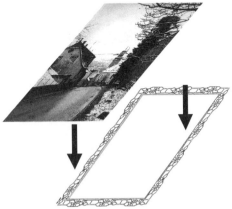

© 1976 Jerry B. Day

Scanning Physical Objects

You can use your HP ScanJet scanner as a camera by scanning actual physical objects such as leaves, coins, jewelry, etc. directly. Objects may be scanned and used as you would a photograph. Pieces of wood, cloth, stone, etc. may be scanned and used as backgrounds.

Caution

Be extremely careful when scanning physical objects. The scanner glass could be scratched or broken. Do not place heavy objects on your scanner. Also, make sure the object does not damage the lid.

Your HP ScanJet scanner has a limited depth-of-field of about two inches. Depth of field is a photographic term describing how much of an object is in focus. The ScanJet can scan objects up to two inches in depth and the object will be in focus. Objects thicker than two inches will have the first two inches in focus and the rest of the object will be out of focus. For example, if you were to scan an object thicker than two inches, say a can of soda, the front part of the can will be in sharp focus, but the rear of the can will have progressively softer focus. You can use this to your advantage as do professional photographers. By having the fore part of the object in focus and the rest out of focus, the fore part will be emphasized.

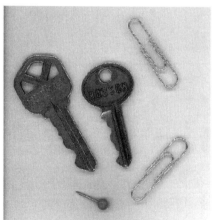

Miscellaneous objects scanned as 256-level grayscale photograph.

Cloth patch scanned as 256-level grayscale photograph.

This technique can be used to produce catalog illustrations of watches, jewelry, badges, medals, etc.—anything that can fit on the scanner glass.

Most real objects scan best as 16-level or 256-level grayscale photographs. Some objects may lend themselves to a special effect by being scanned as a line art drawing.

Leaf scanned as a 256-level grayscale photograph. Brightness set at 170, contrast at 180, sharpening set at normal.

Leaf scanned as a black-and-white drawing. Brightness, contrast and sharpening set at same levels as image on the left.

Scanning Transparent Objects

Interesting effects may be obtained by scanning transparent or translucent objects. Such objects may require increase in brightness for the object to appear translucent or transparent. Such objects may require a bit of experimentation with the brightness and/or contrast controls to obtain the desired effect.

A translucent grid sheet placed between the scanner glass and a photograph. The photograph is diffused by the grid.

© 1977 Jerry Day

Using Scanned Objects as Backgrounds

Materials such as cloth, paper, wood, etc. may be scanned and used as a background pattern for text in word processing or DTP programs or may be imported into painting or drawing programs and used as part of a design. A good source for patterns such as granite, marble, wood, etc. are samples you can obtain from hardware or flooring stores. Textured fabric samples such as burlap, canvas, etc. may be obtained from craft or fabric stores.

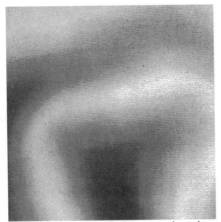

A piece of burlap cloth scanned with no sharpening.

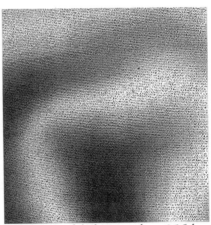

Same piece of cloth scanned as a 256-level grayscale photograph—maximum sharpening applied.

Same piece of cloth shown above used as background for sale advertisement. Scanned image imported into Adobe Photoshop where solarize filter was applied and semi-transparent text added.

Tracing Scanned Objects

Unusual effects can be created by scanning a physical object, then tracing the scan with a drawing program or tracing software.

Tracing the scanned object provides the capability of bringing the object into an illustration program (such as Adobe Illustrator or Aldus Freehand) where the object can be edited and modified. The object's fill pattern can be changed; line widths can be increased or decreased. The object can be reduced, rotated, flipped, or modified in any of the many ways a vector graphic can be manipulated.

A leaf scanned as a 256-level grayscale photograph and traced with Adobe Streamline. The object fill was modified with Adobe Illustrator.

The traced image may be modified in a drawing program. In this example, the original image was copied, reduced, flipped, and fill was changed to produce a second leaf.

Masking Scanned Images

Most image editing or illustration software programs (such as Adobe Photoshop, Aldus PhotoStyler, Adobe Illustrator, CorelDRAW, etc.) have the capability of creating masks that can be placed over scanned images to create special effects.

A 200-dpi, 256-level grayscale scanned image masked with shapes in Adobe Illustrator.
© 1980 Jerry B. Day

A full view of the image shown above without the masking.

Masks may be squares, rectangles, ovals, circles, or irregular shapes. A mask can be used to cover unwanted detail or to create a special "look" for newsletters, marketing materials, or any publication that lends itself to unusual graphic effects.

A 200-dpi, 256-level grayscale EPS file masked with a circle in Adobe Illustrator.
© 1977 Jerry B. Day

A 200-dpi, 256-level grayscale EPS file masked with squares using Adobe Illustrator.
© 1978 Jerry B. Day

Most of these programs allow you to use text as a mask for a scanned image. Consult the user documentation that accompanied your software for instructions on how to create text masks. Many interesting effects can be created with this capability.

A 200-dpi, 256-level grayscale EPS file masked with text in Adobe Illustrator.

© 1978 Jerry B. Day

Where to Obtain Materials for Scanning

Now that you have mastered the techniques of scanning photographs and line art, you may ask "how and from where may I obtain materials to scan?" And the answer is:

- You can make your own photographs. If you are proficient with your equipment, this will be the least expensive way of obtaining current images. If you do make your own photographs, have the prints produced by a professional photo lab. The one-hour photo labs in shopping malls and the photo processing services of drug stores and grocery stores usually do not have the equipment (and in most cases the skill) to produce black-and-white prints. Professional photo labs can produce custom prints with good contrast, and focus, and they can lighten or darken selected areas of the print. A high-quality print will make the scanning process easier and better.

- You can hire a professional photographer to produce photographs for you. If your photographic needs are demanding or unusual, a professional photographer will have equipment and knowledge to satisfy your requirements.

- Historic photographs may be obtained from museums, national, state and local historical societies, and governmental agencies.
  Many of these images are free of copyrights (are in the public domain), but most museums, and historical, and governmental organizations require the payment of reproduction charges and many also charge a usage fee (the fees are based on the number of copies of your publication).

- Historic line art may be obtained from books, magazines, and other material that have expired copyrights.

- Thousands of images are available from commercial clip art books. These images are copyright free and are inexpensive. Most clip art producers have limitations on how many of their images you may use per publication.

Tip:

Copyright law is complicated and involves legal and ethical questions that are beyond the scope of this publication. Before scanning any materials, it is your legal and moral obligation to determine if the materials are protected by copyright laws. Generally, publications older than 75 years are no longer protected by copyrights. Consult an attorney before scanning any historic materials to be sure you are not violating trademarks or copyrights.

See Also

Refer to page 204 for a listing of commercial clip art books.

A historic photograph (circa 1908) obtained from a private collection. Interesting and historic photographs may be obtained from private individuals by advertising in community news publications.   © Jerry B. Day (copyright obtained from original owner)

CHAPTER
8

PRINTING SCANNED IMAGES

Introduction

Some scanned images are intended for display on the screen only—such as online documentation, multi-media, or audio-visual presentations. Most scanned images are printed on paper—either laser output, duplication on a copier, or commercially printed on a press. This chapter shows you how to print your scanned images and how to select the best paper or print medium.

Printing Scanned Images on Laser Printers

Scanned images are normally printed on a desktop or office printer such as a laser printer, or commercially printed using a high-resolution imagesetter and a printing press.

You will, in all likelihood, print your final master pages or proof pages on a 300- or 600-dpi laser printer. Laser printers produce excellent prints of scanned images and in many cases these prints will serve as the masters for duplication on an office copy machine or as CRA (camera-ready-art) masters for commercial printing.

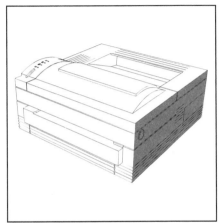

Hewlett-Packard 300-dpi LaserJet 4L printer

Hewlett-Packard 600-dpi LaserJet 4M printer

Your laser printer will probably use one of two computer languages or methods to print your scanned images: Hewlett-Packard's Printer Control Language (PCL) or Adobe System's PostScript. PCL is built-in to every HP LaserJet printer and many laser printers from other manufacturers. PostScript is sometimes built-in or offered as an option, depending on the manufacturer and the particular printer model. Each language offers its own set of advantages and disadvantages and discussion of these is beyond the scope of this book. If you plan to use a high-resolution imagesetter, be aware that most use the PostScript language and documents proofed using PCL may not print correctly on a PostScript device. This is because the two use different typeface and font technology with different character spacing. This could cause layout and pagination problems. Also, PCL printers will not print Encapsulated PostScript (EPS or EPSF) files. If you attempt to print an Encapsulated PostScript file on a PCL printer, either the low-resolution TIFF or PICT file will be printed or nothing will print.

When printing scanned images on a laser printer, you may find the currently available memory in your printer to be insufficient to print scanned images (particularly large grayscale images). Most laser printers are shipped with one to two megabytes of memory built in. This will not be enough memory to print a full-page scanned image. For example, to print a full page scanned image at 600 dpi, you must have a minimum of four megabytes of memory in the printer.

Laser printers that print at 300 dpi will be adequate for many of your scanned images, depending on the type of publication, the audience, the type of image, and whether you are using the 300 dpi output as a proof or as final output.

Laser printers that offer 600 dpi output such as the HP LaserJet 4 and LaserJet 4M, offer significant quality improvements over 300-dpi printers. 300-dpi printers produce 90,000 dots per square inch, whereas 600-dpi printers produce 360,000 dots per inch—*four times* the number of dots. The increase in resolution produces great looking type and eliminates the jaggies in line art. The improvements in scanned grayscale and halftone images is perhaps the most visible improvement. With four times the number of dots to work with, the halftone frequency (lines-per-inch) can be increased from a default of 60 lpi to 85 lpi for PostScript and 106 lpi for PCL5.

The output from 600-dpi printers is of such high quality that it will meet many of your printing requirements without the need to use a high-resolution image-setter. Many publications such as corporate newsletters, newspapers, short press run books, technical illustrations, etc. do not require resolution greater than 600 dpi to be acceptable and look professional. The cost savings of using a 600-dpi printer for your final output can be significant. If you do require the extra quality provided by 1,270- to 3,450-dpi resolution imagesetters, 600-dpi PostScript output is excellent for proofing purposes. The 600-dpi output will look more like the final product than you would get by using a 300-dpi printer for proofing purposes.

Tips for Printing with a Laser Printer

If you use a laser printer for your final output, there are several things you can do to ensure the best possible output:

- Set the toner level in your printer to the minimum level that produces good text and images.

- Use special camera-ready art (CRA) paper when printing your final output.

  See Also

  Refer to page 173 for information on selecting CRA paper

- You may wish to spray your final output with an artists clear matt spray to prevent smudging and to keep the toner from flaking off with handling. See page 173.

Selecting Printer Paper

Your laser or inkjet printer will give you the best image if you use papers that are exceptionally smooth and free of dust, lint, or talc. The smoother and brighter the paper, the sharper your image will be. Talc is used in papers made of cotton fiber. The talc will come off and leave a residue in your printer and will degrade your image quality. Generally, copier papers will not provide the high-quality results that a paper developed specifically for laser and other desktop printers provides.

Qualities to look for in printer paper include:

- The brightest white you can obtain
- Maximum smoothness
- Minimum lint
- Packaging that controls moisture
- Resistance to static build-up
- Specifically developed for desktop or laser printers.

Papers to avoid when using a laser printer or injet printer include:

- Avoid coated papers, either glossy or matt. The coating may melt and damage your printer.
  This caution may not apply to other types of printers, for example: Hewlett-Packard inkjet printers use clay-coated papers.
- Paper heavier than 35 pounds or lighter than 20 pounds. Heavy or lightweight papers can cause printer jams and the lightweight papers may allow images to show through to the other side.
- Papers with foil and letterhead with embossing or printed with thermography. Foil leaf can melt and damage the printer. The embossed letterhead can jam the printer or scratch the drum. Letterhead produced with thermography can also damage the drum or rub off and contaminate the inside of the printer.
- Highly textured paper should be avoided unless you are looking for a special effect. The texture will not produce a sharp scanned image.

If desktop printer output is to be your final copy (you do not plan to use a commercial printer or copier), you will probably wish to use the best paper you can afford to create the best impression.

Selecting Camera-Ready Art Paper

Several paper manufacturers produce special papers for producing camera-ready art (CRA) masters. These papers are usually thicker than normal bond paper and are coated with special materials that make the toner from the laser printer adhere to the papers better than conventional papers. Most of these CRA papers are coated on one side with a wax hold-out material. This material prevents the rubber cement or wax used to mount the masters on boards from bleeding through the paper. High brightness and smooth surface typify this type of paper. These qualities produce the highest contrast possible on a laser printer.

Camera-ready art produced with this type of paper is used to produce masters that are provided to commercial printers for mass production printing on an offset or other type of printing press. To protect these CRA masters, designers often mount each page on stiff card stock to minimize damage while handling the masters. White illustration board may be used for mounting the masters, or special paste-up sheets printed with a non-reproducing blue ink are available from art supply stores. Designers may also spray the masters with a clear artist's spray to further protect them. Another technique used by designers and artists is to attach a transparent cover sheet over the master (tracing paper is often used). This further serves to protect the master and is used to provide instructions to the printer such as to indicate colors for spot printing. A master prepared in this manner is called a "mechanical" by artists, designers, and commercial printers.

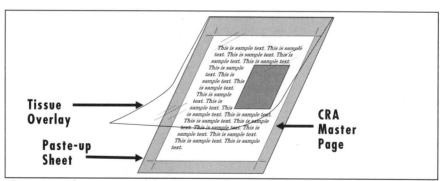

Camera-ready art prepared for commercial printing by mounting the master page on a paste-up sheet and covering it with a tissue overlay.

Most paper manufacturers that produce papers for laser printers produce special proofing or master paper. Several of the manufacturers offer sample or trial packages of their papers for producing masters. Contact office supply stores, art supply shops, or paper distributors for availability and pricing.

These papers are intended to be used as *masters* for duplication by a printer using an offset or other type of printing press. You probably would not wish to use these papers for printing final output on your laser printer as they are more expensive than normal laser paper and some have special markings to indicate the coated side.

Special camera-ready art (CRA) papers are brighter and whiter than the laser or copier paper often used in laser printers. Images such as this winter scene will have more contrast and will seem sharper because the toner will not spread as much as with conventional paper. © 1976 Jerry B. Day

Printing Overhead Transparencies

You may wish to print a scanned image on transparency film to show with an overhead transparency projector to an audience . Transparencies are regularly used in business presentations and by graphic designers and artists to show proposals to clients.

If you plan to print documents containing scanned images on transparency film, use film designed for use with computer printers. Use of a film not designed for printers can have disastrous results—the film may melt and damage your printer. In addition, film not designed for printers may be thicker than printer film. This may create unsharp images and the image may look foggy or misty.

Warning

Do not use copier transparency film on your computer printer. Copier transparency material was not designed for the high heat generated by laser printers.

Several companies offer special transparency material for inkjet or laser printers. Some of the material has a special removable backing that absorbs the heat generated by the printers.

Fail Safe Parachute Company #1

© 1976 Jerry B. Day

Printing Scanned Images on an Imagesetter

You may wish to produce documents or publications at higher resolutions than that provided by 300- or 600-dpi printers. Documents such as annual reports and magazines normally require the highest quality output. The printing budget for such documents usually permits the use of the best materials.

High resolution devices, known as *imagesetters*, allow you to produce CRA masters (including your scanned images) at resolutions from 1,270 to 3,386 dpi. These camera-ready masters can then be used by commercial printers to produce your documents on a printing press. Sometimes these devices are referred to as "typesetters." This is technically incorrect—a "typesetting" machine can only produce text; whereas an "imagesetter" can produce text, line art, and halftoned images.

An imagesetter is similar to the familiar 300- or 600-dpi laser printer; it uses a laser beam to produce images as does the laser printer. The primary difference is, the imagesetter imprints its images on photographic film or resin-coated (RC) paper that must be processed in a separate photo processing machine. Most imagesetters use the Adobe PostScript page description language to produce pages containing text, line art, and halftoned images. PostScript is *device-independent*, meaning that a document printed with PostScript will print at the highest resolution of the printer being used. For example, if you produce a document with a program such as PageMaker or Quark Xpress and print it on your 300- or

A typical high-resolution imagesetter—the Linotype Linotronic Model 300.

600-dpi laser printer, you can send the same document to a service bureau equipped with an imagesetter and get back high-resolution film or resin-coated (RC) paper masters.

Caution

If you plan to produce your master copies using an imagesetter, you should design your document for and proof it on a PostScript printer. Almost all service bureaus use PostScript imagesetters. If you use another type of printer to proof your documents (such as PCL), the document may not print correctly on the imagesetter.

Service Bureaus

High-resolution imagesetters are produced by several manufacturers such as Linotronic and Agfa. Many large companies or government organizations have imagesetters in-house, but most people producing documents with computers use service bureaus. Imagesetters are very expensive (the least costly model is priced over $20,000) and they are difficult to maintain. Service bureaus offer imagesetter services to the general public. Service bureaus may be found almost everywhere; even small towns usually have at least one.

Tip:
The Association of Imaging Service Bureaus is a non-profit association of service bureaus. It publishes a Membership Directory listing service bureaus in the U.S.A. and the equipment they have available. Contact AISB at 1-800-844-AISB.

The service bureau can take the same files you printed on your 300- or 600-dpi PostScript printer and print them on their imagesetter. You have several choices when sending your files to a service bureau:

- If they have the same program (and same version) used to produce your files, you can give them a disk containing the document and image files. They will load the files into their program and print to the imagesetter the same way you print to your printer.

- If they do not have the same program (or the same version) you used to produce your files, you can print the document to a floppy disk (printing documents usually requires several disks). The service bureau does not have to use the same program if you do this.
- You can transmit files to the service bureau with a modem.

Caution

Transmitting large files to a service bureau can be expensive and time consuming. Even with a high-speed modem, files with scanned grayscale or halftone images can be quite large and the transmission time can be many hours. You should consider this option only if there is no service bureau within a reasonable distance.

Printing a File to a Disk

Printing to a floppy disk (the technical term is a *print-to-disk file*) is a method of printing your document to a floppy disk instead of directly to your printer. When you print a document on your PostScript printer, a PostScript file (some call it a PostScript program) is sent to your printer. When producing a print-to-disk file, the same PostScript file that would normally be sent to your printer is recorded in a file on the floppy disk(s). The service bureau can send the file directly to their imagesetter without having to use the same software you used.

See Also

Refer to the user documentation for the software program you are using for instructions on how to *print-to-a-file*. If you are using Microsoft Windows, consult the Windows *User Guide*.

When printing a file to a disk, always print to your hard disk first. Copy the file to a floppy after you check the file size to see if it will fit on a floppy disk.

Note

If the files you create with this method are too large to fit on a floppy disk, try printing the document in segments—a few pages or a single page per file. You can also use a file compression program to reduce the file size.

If you produce high-resolution output on a regular basis, you may wish to investigate the use of an optical disk drive or a removable disk drive such as Bernoulli or SyQuest.

Selecting a Service Bureau

When selecting a service bureau to produce your high-resolution camera-ready art masters be sure to ask the following questions:

- Does it have (and use) the same software you used to produce your files?

- Does the service bureau have the same typefaces (fonts) that you used in your document?

- Does it have file-compression software for the system you are using? (file-compression software is available for both MS-DOS and Macintosh systems).

- What will be done if there is a problem? Some service bureaus are very knowledgeable about desktop publishing, PostScript, and the various software applications. Some have limited knowledge and will not be able to solve a problem with your files. You may be left on your own—a knowledgeable bureau is worth the extra money that they may charge.

- Does the service bureau have both PCs and Macintoshes connected to the imagesetter?

  Note

  Many service bureaus use only Apple Macintosh systems (because PostScript was first available on the Macintosh and early imagesetters worked only with Macintoshes). If you are using a PC and the service bureau does not have a PC connected to the imagesetter, you will have to print a PostScript file on a disk and transfer it to a Macintosh. This works most of the time, but font problems do occur.

- Does it use the same photo processor for film and paper? Different processors for film and RC paper should be used.

- Does it charge by the page or by imagesetter time? Scanned images can be large and take a long time to print on an imagesetter—if the service bureau charges by the imagesetter time, your charges may be high.

- How the imagesetter calibrated? The service bureau should calibrate every job with a densitometer (a device that measures the density of the processed film or paper).

- Does the service bureau's photographic processor use a replenishment or recirculating system?
  Replenishment automatically adds new chemistry when needed and is the best for consistent quality.
- Can it provide proofs from the imagesetter negatives (it is not easy to judge halftones on a negative—even for experienced personnel)?
- Can the service bureau provide a list of references who have used its services?

Service Bureau Check List

Things to Do

☐ Talk to the service bureau staff before you take or send your files to them. Make sure you understand what they want and need from you. They may have suggestions that will help you get the best results. Finding out what their requirements are after you have created your scans and your documents can be costly and painful if you need to make changes.

☐ Make your scanned image files as small as possible (scan at the size used in the final document).

☐ Include all linked graphic files (if you don't, the low-resolution screen image will be printed).
For example, PageMaker uses PICT or TIFF to display EPS graphics on the computer screen. If you do not include the EPS files when you go to the service bureau, the low-resolution PICT or TIFF files will be printed (unless you print the file to a PostScript file).

☐ Take a printout of your document to the service bureau along with the computer files (see the sidebar on LaserCheck software at the end of this chapter).

☐ Make sure you are using the correct printer setup.

Note

Microsoft Windows and the Macintosh operating systems include drivers and PPD (PostScript Printer Description files) for most major imagesetters. Check with your service bureau on which one to use. If you do not have the correct driver or PPD, they can usually be obtained from Microsoft, Apple, or the printer manufacturer.

☐ Be sure to indicate to the service bureau your output requirements or preferences (the suggested list on the next page should provide for most requirements).

Service Bureau Output Preferences

- Paper or Film
  Film is harder to judge, but film eliminates one step in the printing process. A negative must be made from paper output before a printing plate can be produced.

- Positive or Negative
  Most of the time, you will ask for a negative on film. Printing plates are usually made from a film negative.

- Emulsion Up or Down
  The emulsion side of a sheet of film is the dull side. This is the side where the silver emulsion was coated and where the image was recorded. The shiny side is the base of the film.

- Right-Reading
  This means when you look at the film with the emulsion side away from you, you will be able to read the text.

- Orientation—portrait or landscape.
  Portrait is a vertical page, while landscape is a horizontal page. Imagesetter film is wider than most laser printers. Most imagesetters are capable of reorienting your pages, placing portrait pages horizontally on a sheet of film—this saves you money.

- Resolution—(typically from 1,270 to 2,540 or higher).
  The service bureau will probably charge more for higher resolutions. For most black-and-white work 1,270 dpi is adequate. Higher resolutions should be used for four-color separation work.

- Screen Frequency (in lines-per-inch).

- Screen Angle (in degrees).

  Note

  If you do not understand the commercial printing process or are not familiar with the terms discussed above, ask your service bureau or commercial printer to explain them to you. If a service bureau or printer is not readily available, several books listed in the references in Chapter 10 explain service bureaus and commercial printing.

Things to Avoid

- Don't use the PICT format for your scanned images (service bureaus report many problems with PICT files and many refuse to accept them). Use the TIFF or Encapsulated PostScript format.

- Don't expect the service bureau to fix errors that you made such as placing an image on the wrong page—that's the reason for carefully proofing your pages before sending them to the service bureau.

- Do not put large publications into one large print-to-disk file. If the service bureau has a problem with a page or one image, it may not be able to complete your publication.

Note

Service bureaus make money by processing as many pages as possible. If your project will not print, they probably will remove it from their queue. They may attempt to print it again, or they may ask you to redo your print-to-disk files. By sending your publication in several smaller print-to-disk files, you ensure that any problem page or file will be isolated and the rest of the publication will be printed.

Tip:

If you regularly send files to a service bureau, you may wish to purchase LaserCheck from Systems of Meritt. LaserCheck is a software program that uses your 300- or 600-dpi laser printer to emulate a high resolution imagesetter. LaserCheck comes with disks for both Macintosh and MS-DOS PCs. LaserCheck provides a low-cost check of your files before you print them on imagesetter film or RC paper. LaserCheck produces a reduced version of your page on a standard sheet of paper so that you can see if the crop marks are correct. It also provides a list of the fonts used. LaserCheck provides an estimate of imagesetter printing times for each page. If a page will not print, LaserCheck will tell you what is wrong by listing the PostScript error. These are errors not easy to interpret, but you will at least know there is a problem before incurring service bureau charges. You should provide a copy of the LaserCheck printout to the service bureau with your files. It will help them in printing your project.

LaserCheck is available from:

Systems of Meritt, Inc. 2551 Old Dobbin Drive

East Mobile, AL 36695

(205) 660-1240

CHAPTER
9

REAL WORLD SCANNING

Introduction

HP ScanJet scanners are being used by thousands of people all over the world to produce a fantastic variety of publications, ranging from simple newsletters and business presentations to magazines, books, and complex artwork for product packaging. This chapter highlights samples of actual work produced by practical people with HP ScanJet scanners. None of the samples shown here were produced by professional document designers. These examples show individuals using HP ScanJet scanners in real world, down-to-earth situations. Their scanners have given them the power to quickly and easily add the visual to their written materials.

Technical Training Made More Visual with HP Scanners

Ray Ostlie, Vice President of Training for Capstone Electronics of Aurora, Colorado uses many illustrations in the training materials he produces. Capstone is a distributor of electronic components, including passive components (like capacitors and resistors), electromechanical devices (like relays and switches), and connectors. Ostlie produces training materials that help Capstone sales people understand what these components do in electronic circuits, as well as how to help the customer select the best products for their needs.

"Glossary of Capacitor Terms" written by Ray Ostlie, is an electronics industry resource of information about capacitors.

A sample page from "Glossary of Capacitor Terms." Line art illustrations scanned with HP ScanJet Plus and imported into Ventura Publisher.

Capstone Electronics Literature Has Professional Look with Help of HP ScanJets

Capstone offers a product line that includes thousands of electronic components. The training materials (and other technical publications) require detailed illustrations of the components. Ostlie uses HP scanners to produce high-quality materials for use both within Capstone and within the larger electronics industry. He scans black-and-white line art of the components as bitmapped images then imports them into publishing software to add captions and labels. Ostlie cites the improvements in quality: "The things we produce look more professional and have proven to be highly effective training materials. We have hundreds of sales people throughout North America and by using high quality scanned images of line art drawn by artists, our staff is able to recognize the electronic components when they see them on a circuit board. Using scanned images solved a big problem: we used to have to ship samples of all of the different kinds of parts we handle to each sales person so they could learn to recognize them. The HP scanner has eliminated the need for that expensive approach."

More Productive with Scanning

Before acquiring the HP scanners, Capstone produced literature using conventional methods. "Previously the only real alternative was to lay out artwork using the cut-and-paste method and mess around with the copy machine. But photographs never photocopied well and the quality just wasn't there. Using line art and the HP scanners has saved tremendous time in preparation—probably about a two-thirds time savings. And the real savings shows up every time you make changes."

Ray Ostlie's Toolbox

Ostlie uses a 33 mhz 486 PC, Hewlett-Packard ScanJet Plus and ScanJet IIc scanners, HP LaserJet III printer with PostScript, Ventura Publisher and Word-Perfect 5.1.

Italica Press Produces Labors of Love

Throughout the ages, many great book ideas never became reality because the authors could not convince publishing companies to print their books. Today, desktop computers, publishing software, laser printers, and the HP ScanJet have given the power of the press to small presses who wish to publish books that appeal to special markets.

Ron Musto and Eileen Gardiner, a husband and wife team from New York City, established Italica Press in 1986 to produce a series of modern novels, and medieval and Renaissance books. Both are former academics with a love of art and books. Ron has a Ph.D. in medieval history and Eileen a Ph.D. in English literature and comparative literature. They wanted to publish both modern Italian fiction in translation and medieval and Renaissance works. They knew that scholars like themselves would be interested both in new titles and in new editions of classics no longer available to the public. Their new editions would be produced electronically and would be made available at a reasonable price. The new editions would have new bibliographies, new introductions, and would be newly typeset—truly labors of love!

Their latest offering, entitled *Aldus and His Dream Book*, is a biography of and essay about Aldus Manutius, the famous Renaissance scholar and printer (Aldus Inc., producer of PageMaker and other DTP software took their name from Aldus Manutius). Written by American Book Award winner, Helen Barolini, the book follows the layout of a book printed by Aldus Manutius in 1499 entitled *Hypnerotomachia Poliphili* by Francesco Colonna. Several pages of the original 1499 work and all of the illustrations are reproduced in the Italica Press book.

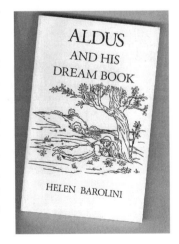

Musto and Gardiner used their HP ScanJet Plus to scan woodcuts from facsimiles of a 1499 edition of *Hypnerotomachia Poliphili*. The images were scanned at 300 dpi, saved in the TIFF format, and imported into Aldus PageMaker. Camera-ready-art masters were produced at 300-dpi on a laser printer. The books are printed at 80 percent of original size. This increases the effective resolution of the text and graphics in the printed books.

Renaissance woodcut from Aldus and His Dream Book. Scanned as black-and-white line art at 300 dpi and saved as a TIFF file.

The 1992 edition of the Italica Press catalog lists 28 titles including modern fiction and medieval and Renaissance titles. Musto and Gardiner have produced about six titles per year since beginning Italica in 1986. They have recently begun to produce electronic books on floppy disks.

Italica Press Toolbox

Musto and Gardiner use an Apple Macintosh SE30 with Radius Accelerator, Apple Laserwriter IIg, Hewlett-Packard ScanJet Plus, Microsoft Word, and Aldus PageMaker 4.0.

Each page in Aldus and His Dream Book is a replica of a page from the Aldus Manutius Renaissance classic, Hypnerotomachia Poliphili—*considered to be the most beautiful book printed in the Renaissance.*

Scanning and Tracing Used to Produce Miniature Trains

The *San Juan Car Company* of Union City, California produces highly detailed plastic scale model kits of historic Colorado narrow gauge trains. Owner John Parker uses an HP ScanJet IIp scanner and Adobe Streamline tracing software to produce drawings for the instruction sheets included in the model kits. He also uses his HP ScanJet to scan and trace historic railroad blueprints. The traced drawings are loaded into AutoCAD drafting software, scaled according to ¼-inch equals one foot, and used to design the plastic parts molds.

San Juan Car Company scale model of Denver & Rio Grande Western railroad flanger (a type of snow plow).

© San Juan Car Company

San Juan Car Company's ScanJet IIp scanner and Adobe Streamline tracing software have eliminated drawing by hand and manual paste-up of the kit instruction sheets. Producing the illustrations electronically gives San Juan the flexibility to make changes to the drawings without having to paste-up the instruction sheets again.

Since adapting this new procedure, the San Juan Car Company has significantly reduced the time required to produce the plastic parts molds and reduced the time needed to produce the kit instruction sheets by one-third ". . . and we are producing better looking instruction sheets!" says Parker.

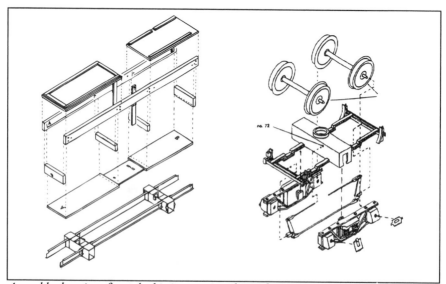

Assembly drawings from the kit instruction sheet of a San Juan Car Company model. Scanned with the HP ScanJet IIp and traced with Adobe Streamline. Drawings were modified and scaled in AutoCAD and imported into Microsoft Word for Windows.
© San Juan Car Company

San Juan Car Company's Toolbox

John Parker uses a Hewlett-Packard Vectra 25 mhz 386 PC, HP LaserJet III printer, HP ScanJet IIp scanner, Microsoft Word for Windows 2.0, Adobe Streamline3.0, ZSoft Photofinish, and AutoDesk AutoCad.

CHAPTER

10

REFERENCES

Introduction

The references listed on the following pages provide additional information on HP ScanJet scanners and the art of desktop scanning. Also included is a list of many software applications that you may use with your HP ScanJet scanner.

Several of the periodicals are available free-of-charge to qualified subscribers. Contact the publishers at the address listed. It is impossible to assure the availability of publications and the accuracy of addresses shown.

Clip art books may be obtained from art supply stores or directly from the producers listed on page 204.

Books

ScanJet Unlimited
By Steve Roth, Chris Dickman, and Salvatore Parascandolo
Peachpit Press, 1990
2414 Sixth Street
Berkeley, CA 94710
☎ (800) 283-9444

The Verbum Book of Scanned Imagery
By Michael Gosney, Linna Dayton, and Phil Inje Chang
M&T Books, 1991
Redwood City, CA 94063
☎ (415) 366-3600

The Gray Book
By Michael Gosney
Ventana Press, 1990
P.O. Box 2468
Chapel Hill, NC 27515
☎ (919) 942-0220

The Complete Scanner Handbook for Desktop Publishing
and *The Complete Scanner Toolbook*
(separate PC and Mac versions are available)
By David D. Busch
Business One Irwin, 1992
Homewood, IL 60430-1795
☎ (800) 634-3966 extension 828

The Scanner Book
By Stephen Beale and James Cavuto
Micro Publishing Press
21150 Hawthorne Blvd., Suite 104
Torrance, CA 90503
☎(310) 371-5787

The Legal Guide for the Visual Artist
North Light Books
1507 Dana Avenue
Cincinnati, OH 45207
☎(800) 289-0963

Everyone's Guide to Successful Publications
By Elizabeth W. Adler
Peachpit Press, 1993
2414 Sixth Street
Berkley, CA 94710
☎(800) 283-9444

The Verbum Book of Digital Painting
and
The Verbum Book of Electronic Page Design
Verbum, 1991
P.O. Box 12564
San Diego, CA 92112
☎(619) 233-9977

WYSIWYG: How to make sure that what you see is the same as what you get!
By Peter Fink
Peachpit Press, 1993
2414 Sixth Street
Berkley, CA 94710
☎(800) 283-944493

Looking Good In Print
By Roger C. Parker
Ventana Press
P.O. Box 2468
Chapel Hill, NC 27515
☎(919) 942-0220

Design Essentials: Professional Studio Techniques
Adobe Press
Prentice Hall Computer Publishing, 1992
11711 North College Avenue
Carmel, IN 46032
☎(800) 428-5331

Copyrighted Content: The Cautious Editor's Guide to Using Printed Material
and
Things Your Printer Might Tell You (or Not)
Promotional Perspectives
Publications Division
1955 Pauline Blvd.
Suite 100-A
Ann Arbor, MI 48103-5003
☎(313) 996-3970

Linotronic Imaging Handbook
By James Cavuoto and Stephen Beale
Micro Publishing Press, 1990
21150 Hawthorne Blvd., Suite 104
Torrance, CA 90503
☎(213) 371-5787

Pocket Pal : A graphic arts production handbook
International Paper Company, 1992
P.O. Box 100, Church Street Station
New York, NY 10008-0100
☎ (212) 431-5222

Macworld Photoshop 2.5 Bible
By Deke McClelland
IDG Books 1992
155 Bovet Road
San Mateo, CA 94402
☎ (800) 762-2974

The Official Adobe Photoshop Handbook
By David Biedny and Bert Monroy
The Color Resource
708 Montgomery Street
San Francisco, CA 94111-2104
☎ (800) 827-3311

The Photoshop Wow! Book
By Linnea Dayton and Jack Davis
Peachpit Press, 1993
2414 Sixth Street
Berkeley, CA 94710
☎ (800) 283-9444

Designer Photoshop
By Rob Day
Random House Electronic Publishing, 1993
400 Hahn Road
Westminster, MD 21157
☎ (800) 733-3000

Seybold Professional Guide to Adobe Photoshop
By Peter Fink
Ziff-Davis Press, 1993
5903 Christie Avenue
Emeryville, CA 94608
☎(800) 688-0448

The Photoshop 2.5 Designer's Guide
By Wayde Gardner
Sybex, Inc., 1993
2021 Challenger Drive
Alameda, CA 94501
☎(800) 227-2346

Mastering Aldus PhotoStyler
By Sybil and Emil Ihrig
The Color Resource
708 Montgomery Street
San Francisco, CA 94111-2104
☎(800) 827-3311

Illustrator Illuminated
By Clay Andres
Peachpit Press, 1992
2414 Sixth Street
Berkley, CA 94710
☎(800) 283-9444

Illustration Techniques with Adobe Illustrator For Windows
By Linda Miles and Betty Wilson
Hayden Publishing Company, 1992
11711 North College Avenue
Carmel, IN 46032
☎(317) 573-6880

Power of Adobe Illustrator for Windows
By David Holtzgang
MIS Press/Henry Holt, 1992
115 West 18th Street
New York, NY 10011
☎(800) 628-9658

The Adobe Illustrator 5.0 Designer's Guide
By Deke McClelland
Sybex, Inc., 1993
2021 Challenger Drive
Alameda, CA 94501
☎(800) 227-2346

Mastering CorelDRAW "Special Edition"
By Rick Altman
Sybex, Inc., 1993
2021 Challenger Drive
Alameda, CA 94501
☎(800) 227-2346

Mastering CorelDRAW, 3rd Edition
By Chris Dickman
Peachpit Press, 1993
2414 Sixth Street
Berkley, CA 94710
☎(510) 548-4393

Power of CorelDRAW
By Jim Karney
MIS Press/Henry Holt, 1992
115 West 18th Street
New York, NY 10011
☎(800) 628-9658

Looking Good with CorelDRAW
By Nemoy and Aiken
Ventana Press
P.O. Box 2468
Chapel Hill, NC 27515
☎(919) 942-0220

Inside CorelDRAW
By Daniel Gray and Steve Shubitz
New Rivers Publishing
1171 N. College Avenue, Sute 140
Carmel, IN 46032

Periodicals

Aldus Magazine
411 First Avenue S.
Seattle, WA 98104
☎(206) 622-5500

Business Publishing
P.O. Box 5019
Brentwood, TN 37024-9846
☎(708) 665-1000

Before & After
1830 Sierra Gardens Drive, Suite 30
Roseville, CA 95661
☎(916) 784-3880

Color Publishing
P.O. Box 3184
Tulsa, OK 74101
☎(508) 392-2157

Computer Graphics World
P.O. Box 21638
Tulsa, OK 74121-9980
☎(918) 835-3161 ext. 400

Corel Magazine
Ariel Communications, Inc..
P.O. Box 202380
Austin, TX 78720-9888
☎(512) 250-1700

Desktop Communications
P.O. Box 941745
Atlanta, GA 30341
☎(800) 966-9052

EC&I (Electronic Composition & Imaging)
505 Consumers Road, Suite 102
Willowdate, Ontario
Canada M2J9Z9
☎(416) 299-6007

MacArtist
P.O. Box 361
Santa Ana, CA 92702
☎(818) 760-8983

MAC WORLD
and *PC WORLD*
Subscription Department
P.O. Box 51666
Boulder, CO 80321-1666
☎(415) 243-0505

MAC User Magazine
and *Windows User Magazine*
Ziff-Davis Publishing Company
1 Park Avenue
New York, NY 10016
☎(800) 627-2247

NADTP Journal
National Association of Desktop Publishers
462 Old Boston Street
Topsfield, MA 01983-9900

Corelation
Association of Corel Artists &
Designers
2912 3rd Street, Suite 4
Santa Monica, California 90405
☎(310) 452-5637

PC Publishing and Presentations
P.O. Box 941909
Atlanta, GA 30341-9958
☎(800) 966-9052

Photo Electronic Imaging
New Subscription Department
1090 Executive Way
Des Plaines, IL 60018-1587
☎(708) 299-8161

Publish
Subscriber Services
P.O. Box 55400
Boulder, CO 80322
☎(800) 274-5116

Step-by-Step Electronic Design
Dynamic Graphics, Inc.
6000 N. Forest Park Drive
Peoria, IL 61614-3592
☎(800) 255-8800

The Page
661 Roscoe Street
Chicago, IL 60657-2926

Verbum Magazine
P.O. Box 15439
San Diego, CA 92115
☎(619) 233-9977

Windows Style
P.O. Box 941745
Atlanta, GA 30341-9958
☎(404) 908-5744

Clip Art Sources

ARTmaster
500 N. Claremont Blvd.
Claremont, CA 91711
☎(714) 626-8065

Dover Publications
31 East 2nd Street
Mineola, NY 11501
☎(516) 294-7000

Dynamic Graphics, Inc.
60000 North Forest Park Dr.
P.O. Box 1901
Peoria, IL 61666-1901
☎(800) 255-8800

Scanned as a 300-dpi TIFF file, traced with Corel TRACE.
© Dover Publications

Scanned as a 300-dpi TIFF file, traced with Adobe Streamline.
© Dynamic Graphics

Graphic Products Corporation
Rolling Meadows, IL 60008

Dick Sutphen Studio
P.O. Box 38
Malibu, CA 90265
☎(818) 889-1575

The Church Art Works
875 High Street, N.E.
Salem, OR 97301
☎(503) 370-9377

Volk Clip Art
P.O. Box 347
Washington, IL 61571-0347
☎(800) 227-7048

Scanned as a 300-dpi TIFF file, traced with Corel TRACE.

© Volk Clip Art

Scanned as 300-dpi TIFF file, traced with Adobe Streamline.

© Graphic Products Corporation

Software Applications

Following are lists of many of the currently available software applications that you may use with your HP ScanJet scanner. You should be able to use any software application that can import one of the HP ScanJet scanner supported file formats (TIFF, EPS, PICT, etc.). For more information about these products, contact the companies listed.

See Also

Refer to Chapter 3 for information on selecting a file format.

Desktop Publishing Applications

Application	Computer System	Company	Phone Number
Aldus PageMaker	Windows, Macintosh	Aldus Corp.	(206) 628-2320
Aldus Personal Press	Macintosh	Aldus Corp. (Silicon Beach)	(619) 695-6956
Express Publisher for DeskMate	DOS	Power Up Software Corp.	(415) 345-5900
The Forms	DOS	The Top Banana, Inc.	(714) 449-7777
FrameMaker	Windows, Macintosh	Frame Technology, Inc.	(800) U4-FRAME
MaxPage	Macintosh	Applied Systems Technology	(315) 675-8584
Microsoft Publisher	Windows	Microsoft Corp.	(800) 227-4679
Publish It Easy	Macintosh	Timeworks, Inc.	(708) 559-1300
QuarkXPress	Windows, Macintosh	Quark, Inc.	(303) 934-2211
Ready, Set, Go	Macintosh	Letraset	(800) 343-TYPE
Ventura Publisher	DOS/GEM, Windows, Macintosh	Ventura Software Inc.	(800) 822-8221

Image Scanning and Enhancement

Application	Computer System	Company	Phone Number
Adobe Photoshop	Windows, Macintosh	Adobe Systems, Inc.	(800) 833-6687
Adobe Illustrator	Windows, Macintosh	Adobe Systems, Inc.	(800) 833-6687
Aldus Digital Darkroom	Macintosh	Aldus (Silicon Beach)	(619) 695-6956
Aldus Gallery Effects	Windows, Macintosh	Aldus (Silicon Beach)	(619) 695-6956
Aldus PhotoStyler	Windows	Aldus Corp.	(206) 628-2320
Aldus PrePrint	Windows, Macintosh	Aldus Corp.	(206) 628-2320
Aldus SuperPaint	Macintosh	Aldus Corp.	(619) 695-6965
Canvas 3	Macintosh	Deneba Software	(305) 594-6965
Claris CAD	Macintosh	Claris Corp.	(408) 727-8227
CLAUDIUS	DOS	CPT Corp.	(612) 949-1709
CLEOPATRA	DOS	CPT Corp.	(612) 949-1709
ColorLab	Windows	Computer Presentations, Inc.	(513) 281-3222
ColorStudio	Macintosh	Fractal Design Corp.	(408) 688-8800

Image Scanning and Enhancement *continued...*

Application	Computer System	Company	Phone Number
CorelDRAW	Windows	Corel Systems Corp.	(613) 728-8200, ext. 1857
DeskPaint	Macintosh	Zedcor, Inc.	(800) 482-4567
DeskDraw	Macintosh	Zedcor, Inc.	(800) 482-4567
Enhance	Macintosh	MicroFrontier	(800) 388-8109
Color IT	Macintosh	MicroFrontier	(800) 388-8109
FreeHand	Windows, Macintosh	Aldus Corp.	(206) 628-2320
HALO Desktop Imager	Windows	Media Cybernetics	(800) 992-HALO
Image-In Color	Windows	Image-In, Inc.	(800) 345-3540
Image-In Color Professional	Windows	Image-In, Inc.	(800) 345-3540
Image Plus VCD	DOS	Warley Engineering, Inc.	(305) 351-0083
Imaging for Data Ease	DOS	Solana Software	(619) 291-1533
MacPaint	Macintosh	Claris Corp.	(408) 727-8227
MacDraw Pro	Macintosh	Claris Corp.	(408) 727-8227
Ofoto	Windows, Macintosh	Light Source, Inc.	(800) 231-7226

Image Scanning and Enhancement *continued...*

Application	Computer System	Company	Phone Number
PC Paintbrush	DOS	ZSoft Corp.	(404) 428-0008
Perfect Exposure PF	Windows	Arbor Image Corp.	(313) 741-8700
Picture Publisher	Windows	Micrografx Inc.	(800) 733-3729, ext. 5050
Pixie Imaging Toolbox	DOS	CPT Corp.	(612) 949-1709
Publisher's Paintbrush	Windows	ZSoft Corp.	(404) 428-0008
PhotoFinish	Windows	ZSoft Corp.	(404) 428-0008
The Right Imaging Option	DOS	Tri Software, Inc.	(206) 488-4833
Scan-Do	DOS, Windows	HammerLab	(203) 624-0000
Scan N Clean	DOS, Windows	Artistic Visions, Inc.	(408) 378-1444
ScanTastic	Macintosh	Second Glance Software	(714) 855-2331
Touch-Up	DOS	Migraph, Inc.	(800) 223-3729
Ventura ColorPro	Windows	Ventura Software, Inc.	(800) 822-8221
Ventura PicturePro	Windows	Ventura Software, Inc.	(800) 822-8221

Image Scanning and Enhancement *continued*...

Application	Computer System	Company	Phone Number
Ventura Scan	Windows	Ventura Software, Inc.	(800) 822-8221
Wasatch Portfolio	DOS	Wasatch Computer Technology	(801) 575-8043
WinRix	Windows	PIX Softworks, Inc.	(800) 345-9059
XFormer	DOS	Elcee Computek, Inc.	(407) 750-8061

Optical Character Recognition

Application	Computer System	Company	Phone Number
AccuText	Macintosh	Xerox Imaging Systems, Inc.	(800) 248-6550
Foreign Translation System	DOS	GlobaLink, Inc.	(800) 255-5660
MacReader Japan	Macintosh	Media Drive Lab	485-24-0501 (Japan only)
NestorReader	Windows, DOS	Nestor, Inc.	(401) 331-9640
OmniPage	Windows, DOS	Caere Corp.	(408) 395-7000
OmniPage Professional	Windows	Caere Corp.	(408) 395-7000
Paper Keyboard	Windows, Macintosh	Datacap, Inc.	(914) 347-7133
PERCEIVE	Windows, DOS, Macintosh	Ocron, Inc.	(408) 980-8900
READ-IT! OCR PRO	Windows, Macintosh	OLDUVAI Corp.	(305) 665-4665
ReadRight	Windows, DOS, Macintosh	OCR Systems, Inc.	(800) 233-4627
ReadStar 6	Windows, Macintosh	Inovatic	(703) 522-3053
ReadStar Pro	Windows, Macintosh	Inovatic	(703) 522-3053

Optical Character Recognition *continued*…

Application	Computer System	Company	Phone Number
Recognita Plus	Windows, DOS	Recognita Corp. of America	(800) 255-GOCR
Remark Office OMR	Windows	Principia Products	(800) 853-0860
TextPert	Windows, Macintosh	CTA, Inc.	(800) 252-1442
TextScan 4.0	Macintosh	Prism Enterprises	(301) 604-6611
TrueScan	DOS	Calera Recognition Systems, Inc.	(408) 720-0999
TypeReader	Windows, Macintosh	ExperVision, Inc.	(800) 732-3897
WordScan, WordScan Plus	Windows, Macintosh	Calera Recognition Systems, Inc.	(408) 720-0999

Presentation Graphics

Application	Computer System	Company	Phone Number
Aldus Persuasion	Windows, Macintosh	Aldus Corp.	(206) 628-2320
DrawPerfect	DOS	WordPerfect Corp.	(800) 451-5151
FreeLance Graphics for Windows	Windows	Lotus Development Corp.	(800) 831-9679
Harvard Graphics	Windows, DOS	Software Publishing Corp.	(408) 988-7518
Hollywood	Windows	Claris Corp.	(403) 727-8227
Microsoft Powerpoint	Windows, Macintosh	Microsoft Corp.	(800) 227-4679
SoftCraft Presenter	Windows	SoftCraft, Inc.	(800) 351-0500

Word Processing

Application	Computer System	Company	Phone Number
Ami Pro	Windows	Lotus Development Corp.	(800) 831-9679
DisplayWrite	DOS	IBM Corp.	(800) IBM-7699
MacWrite II	Macintosh	Claris Corp.	(408) 727-8227
Microsoft Word	Windows, DOS, Macintosh	Microsoft Corp.	(800) 227-4679
Multi-Lingual Scholar	DOS	Gamma Products	(213) 394-8622
WordPerfect	Windows, DOS, Macintosh	WordPerfect Corp.	(800) 451-5151
WordStar for Windows	Windows	WordStar International	(800) 227-5609

Specialized Applications

Application	Description	Computer System	Company and Phone Number
APEX	Interferogram analysis program for testing lenses and optical instruments	DOS	Telic Optics, Inc. (508) 485-4088
Arkenstone Reader	Complete hardware and software reading solution for the blind or visually impaired	Windows, DOS	Arkenstone, Inc. (800) 444-4443
ASA 2000	Measurement, sheet analyzer for defects	DOS	Applied Vision Systems, (404) 932-5156
Best Deal	Computerizes promotional allowance forms used by food brokers and manufacturers	DOS	Key Programs, Inc. (305) 753-2752
CASmate	Computer-aided sign making system software with automatic vectorization	Windows, DOS, Macintosh	ScanVel Marketing, Inc. (800) 866-6227
Compu-Fit	3d foot scanning and product selection for ski boots, running, and other shoes	DOS	Foot Image Technology (503) 389-8844
CU/IMAGE	Allows storage of shipping documents on DEC VAX	Windows	Computers Unlimited (406) 255-9500

Specialized Applications *continued...*

Application	Description	Computer System	Company and Phone Number
CNC Machine Support	Scanning and recognition software for generating CNC machine code	Macintosh	Diversified Control, Inc. (716) 822-0700
DocuRead IDB	Software interface designed for blind or visually impared users for use with OCR products	DOS	Adhoc Reading Systems, Inc. (908) 254-7310
Dragon/ips	Scientific; image processing remote sensing software	Windows, DOS	Guldin-Rudah Systems (413) 253-7340
Letter Art	Sign making and lettering software	DOS	Symbol Graphics (714) 736-4040
NGRAVE	2D artwork to 3D machine tool path generation program	DOS	Boston Digital Corp. (508) 473-4561
PaediaScan 1D	1D and 2D DNA sequencing software	Windows, DOS, Macintosh	Paedia Corp. (415) 861-8097
ParTest Biotech	Item banking and test generation software	DOS	Economics Research, Inc. (714) 641-3955
RXSCAN	Hospital prescription routing software	Windows, DOS	Prospect Software (914) 686-9822

Specialized Applications *continued...*

Application	Description	Computer System	Company and Phone Number
Scanbase API	Programming interface to scanners and image processing	DOS	Scanbase Graphics, Inc. (908) 536-9653
Sensorex	Automated data entry software	DOS	Softex, Inc. (717) 397-8875
Skunkworks Scorecard	Tennis statistics analysis software	DOS	Statistics and Demographics (407) 743-1235
Social Secretary	Printing and calligraphy software for flyers and invitations	DOS	Social Secretary (212) 956-2707
SoftScan	Two-dimensional bar-code decoding software	DOS	Softstrip, Inc. (203) 597-9762
Victor Image Processing Library	Image processing library for CC++ programmers	DOS	Catenary Systems (314) 962-7833
Weaselgraphics	Electronic engineering software	DOS	Weaselgraphics (800) 356-8113

Utilities

Application	Description	Computer System	Company and Phone Number
ALICE Image Compression	JPEG image compression	Windows, DOS	Telephoto Communications (619) 452-0903
Arbor Scan	Scan conversion from bitmap to CAD format	DOS	Arbor Image Corp. (313) 677-2280
Auto Image	Raster to vector conversion	DOS	Palisades Research (310) 459-7528
CAD OverLay ESP; OverLay GS; OverLay Classic	Allows display, editing, and plotting of scanned raster images within AutoCAD	DOS	Image Systems Technology, Inc. (518) 283-8783
Capture	Screen capture	Macintosh	Mainstay (818) 991-6540
DocTools	Image scanning, printing, and viewing	DOS	Logo Systems, International (408) 438-5012
Draftsman PF	Raster to vector conversion	Windows, DOS	Arbor Image Corp. (313) 741-8700
FastDraw	Raster to vector converted polyline editor	Windows	Arbor Image Corp. (313) 741-8700
Flipper Graphics Library	A graphics library for the Nantucket Clipper Compiler	DOS	ProWorks (503) 567-1459

Utilities *continued...*

Application	Description	Computer System	Company and Phone Number
Foto Fast and Foto Flyer	Desktop publishing text and image scanning utilities	Windows, DOS	Interproject, Inc. (301) 975-0184
Host	Allows downloading of mainframe data, scanning of overlay documents, storage to optical disk, and printing	DOS	Technet of Tennessee (615) 259-2901
LogoScan	Raster to vector conversion	Windows, DOS	Arbor Image Corp. (313) 741-8700
ScanPro	Vectorizing utility that can convert PCX or DOS TIFF files to DXF or DCII formats	DOS	American Small Business Computers, Inc. (918) 825-4844
Adobe Streamline	Tracing (raster to vector file conversion)	Windows, Macintosh	Adobe Systems, Inc. (800) 833-6683

Document Management

Application	Computer System	Company	Phone Number
ClarisWorks	Windows, DOS	Claris Corp	408) 727-8227
Custom Image Databases	Macintosh	Nexus Technology, Inc.	619) 674-6910
DSS Manager	Windows, DOS	Document Storage Systems, Inc.	(303) 680-3346
E_Quip Private	Windows	Alacrity Systems, Inc.	(908) 813-2501
Exhibit-Link	DOS	InVzn Corp.	(800) 828-8884
File Magic, File Magic Plus, File Magic Plus Professional	Windows	Westbrook Technologies, Inc.	(800) 949-3453 (203) 399-7111
File Plus Lite, File Plus Professional	Windows	GreenGage	408) 243-8960
Group File	Windows	LaserData, Inc.	(508) 649-4600
IMARA, IMARA Lite	Windows	IMARA Research Corp.	(416) 581-1740
Image Fast	Windows	Image Fast Software Systems	(703) 893-7499

Document Management *continued...*

Application	Computer System	Company	Phone Number
Keyfile	Windows	Keyfile Corp.	(603) 883-3800
LaserFiche Executive, LaserFiche NLM	Windows	Compulink Management Center	(310) 212-5465
Legend	Windows, DOS	Document Storage Systems, Inc.	(303) 757-1455
OPTIX Document Imaging System	Macintosh	Blueridge Technologies	(703) 675-3015
PageKeeper	Windows	Caere Corp.	(408) 395-7000
PaperLess Filer	DOS	PaperLess Corporation	(800) 658-6486
QuickView Jr., QuickView Plus, QuickView Manager	Windows, DOS	Seabreeze Engineering, Inc.	(800) 277-3086 (407) 321-2096
ShortCut	DOS, Macintosh	Seabreeze Engineering, Inc.	(800) 277-3086 (407) 321-2096
ViewBase	DOS, Macintosh	Image Systems	(518) 283-8783

Image Enabling

Application	Computer System	Company	Phone Number
Doceo	Windows	Keyfile	(603) 883-3800
Lotus Notes	Windows	Lotus Development Corp.	(617) 577-8500
PaperClip for Windows	Windows	PaperClip Imaging Software, Inc.	(210) 487-3503
Watermark Discovery	Windows	Watermark Software	(617) 229-2600

GLOSSARY

This glossary includes both scanning terminology terms used in this book as well as terms from the photography, publishing, and printing worlds. I have tried to include words and topics that are probably not familiar to those who are new to the publishing and printing fields. For more information on some of these topics, refer to the list of books that may be found in chapter 10.

Automatic Exposure   A feature of the DeskScan II software that automatically sets the contrast and brightness values to optimize the final image quality.

Automatic Find   A feature of DeskScan II software that automatically creates a selection area around the Preview image and adjusts the exposure.

auto trace   A feature of illustration and tracing software that automatically traces bitmapped images and converts them to a vector format.

brightness   A measure of the overall intensity of an image. The lower the brightness (minimum 0), the closer to black the image will be; the higher the brightness (maximum 250), the closer to white the image will be.

bitmap   An arrangement of computer bits that defines an image dot-by-dot.

CAD   Abbreviation of *Computer-Aided Design*. A type of drawing software used by drafting personnel, engineers, industrial designers. Usually found on high-end computer workstations, but also available on Windows and Macintosh systems.

calibration   A process that adjusts the black-and-white values in the image to compensate for changes that software packages and printers make to these values. The purpose of calibration is to ensure accurate and consistent results.

camera-ready art (CRA)   Finished document pages ready to be photographed and printed.

CCD   Charged Couple Device. An important part of the HP ScanJet scanner. It measures the light reflecting from the original image.

compression   A method of reducing the file size of an image so that it requires less disk storage space and computer memory. The DeskScan II software can compress TIFF and PICT images.

contrast   The range between the lightest and darkest shades in an image. A high contrast image has few gray shades between black and white; a low contrast image has more gray shades.

cropping   Selecting a portion of an image.

densitometer   An electronic device that measures the density of an image by measuring the light reflectance or transmittance of the image tones.

dialog box   A window in a program that requests more information from computer users or allows them to choose among options.

diffusion   A halftone type that simulates grayscale. The dots in the image are distributed in a random pattern resulting in excellent image detail and good image texture.

dithering   The method of using dots of different sizes to simulate gray scale images. Large dots grouped close together represent shadow areas, while small dots further apart represent highlight areas.

dot gain   Spreading of ink on the paper surface when printing. Each printing dot grows larger because of the spreading of the ink. Dot gain causes the image to become darker and sometimes less sharp. Dot gain is expressed as a percentage.

DPI   Abbreviation of *dots-per-inch*, the measurement normally used for the resolution of scanners and printers. It is a measure of the number of dots in a square inch. A 300 dpi printer will produce 90,000 dots in a square inch.

drawing   An image with large areas of black and white.

driver   A program that allows the operating system to communicate with a peripheral device.

DTP   Abbreviation of *desktop publishing*. The term was first used by Paul Brainard, founder of Aldus Corporation, developer of the PageMaker program. Desktop publishing is the production of documents using personal computers and page layout (or sophisticated word processing) software.

Encapsulated PostScript   A picture and graphic file format developed by Adobe Systems. It is a form of PostScript for single images or graphics. On MS-DOS systems it is known as "EPS" and on Macintosh systems as "EPSF." Encapsulated PostScript files will only print on a PostScript printer.

file format   The format in which an image is saved. The file format determines which applications can access an image.

FPO   Abbreviation of "For Position Only." A term used by graphic artists, illustrators, and page layout specialists to describe a process in which scanned images are placed temporarily on in a page layout to indicate where the image should go in the final printing. This temporary image may be replaced by a higher resolution scanned image or the image may be stripped in conventionally.

grayscale   The measure of grayness of any area of a picture. Grayscale is one of the image types supported by the HP DeskScan II software. When a picture is scanned, the gray level of each pixel of the image is determined and sent to the computer. Dithered images or halftones are not grayscale; they are a type of line art that creates an impression of gray.

halftone   An image type consisting of black dots on a white base which simulates grayscale by varying the sizes of the dots printed. Black areas consist of large black dots, while lighter areas consist of smaller black dots.

halftone dot   Different sized black shapes created by turning on and off particular spots during printing—either on a laser printer or imagesetter or on a printing press. Halftone dots are shapes that repeat at a regular angle. This repeating pattern produces the illusion of continuous tone. Halftone dots are not the same as printer dots.

highlight   The brightest portion of the original or reproduction that has no color cast. In the highlight area, a printer will print either the smallest printable dot or no dots.

imagesetter   A computer-driven device that produces very high resolution text and images on film or photosensitive paper for reproduction.

image type   The way an image will be scanned and/or reproduced. The black-and-white image types available in DeskScan II software are drawings (or line art), halftones, and photos.

inkjet printer   A type of desktop printer that prints by spraying ink on paper. Inkjet printers can print in black-and-white and color in varying resolutions.

inverting   Process of changing a positive image to a negative image or a negative to a positive.

JPEG Abbreviation of Joint Photographers Experts Group. A standard for compressing and decompressing graphic files.

line art Images with no shades of gray, consisting of black-and-white only—line drawings for example

line screen A measure of the distance between centers of halftone dots, as they repeat along the screen angle (also known as screen ruling). The number of halftone dots that can be in a square inch. Measured in lpi (lines-per-inch).

Live Preview A feature of the DeskScan II software that updates the image in the Preview area to represent the changes made in scanner settings.

macro Small computer programs that record keystrokes or mouse action. Macros can be replayed to automate repetitive tasks.

masking An option in many paint and drawing programs that uses an opaque image to block (mask) parts of a scanned image.

matrix The square grid that forms each halftone dot.

megabyte A measurement of file size or of computer memory equal to 1024 kilobytes (or 1,048,576 bytes).

midtones The gray shades in a continuous tone or halftone image generally between 30 percent and 70 percent black.

moiré Interference patterns that can occur when a halftone image is scanned or when it is scaled in an application after it is scanned.

offset printing A method of commercial printing. A page is photographed and the negative used to produce a metal plate. The plate is attached to a revolving cylinder. Ink is then applied to the plate and transferred to a rubber blanket attached to another cylinder. The paper is passed over this blanket where it is transferred (or offset) to the paper.

OCR Abbreviation for "optical character recognition." Technique of scanning text and converting the resulting image from a bitmapped image to an editable text format.

PCL   Abbreviation of Printer Control Language. Computer language developed by Hewlett-Packard for communications between computers and LaserJet printers.

PCX   Abbreviation for PC Paintbrush Extension. Image file format developed by ZSoft Corporation. One of the first graphic file formats for MS-DOS computers.

PICT   Abbreviation of PICTure. Image file format developed for the original Macintosh computer. PICT images may be bitmaps or vector files.

picture element, pel, or pixel   In computer graphics, the smallest element of a display that can be assigned independent color and intensity. Or, the area of finest detail that can be reproduced on the recording medium. A pixel is one dot on the computer screen.

posterization   A high-contrast special effect created by limiting the number of shades of gray.

PostScript   A computer language developed by Adobe Systems for printing text, graphics and scanned images. PostScript is a vector format that can also include scanned bitmapped images.

Preview Scan   A feature of the DeskScan II software that quickly scans the original at the resolution of the computer screen so that you may select portions of the image (crop) or use the DeskScan tools to enhance the scanned image.

raster graphic   A graphic image consisting of a dot-by-dot representation of the original.

resolution   A measure of how many dots-per-inch (dpi) are scanned or printed. The greater the number of dots-per-inch, the greater amount of detail is visible in the image. The resolution of the image is limited by the capability of the printer or monitor and the scanner. For example, if an image is scanned at 300 dpi and is printed at 150 dpi, the best possible resolution is 150 dpi.

RC   Abbreviation of *Resin Coated*. The type of photographic paper used in high-resolution imagesetters.

screen   Used in conventional halftoning. A sheet of glass or acetate with tiny patterns that act as lenses through which an image is photographed to produce a halftone.

screen angle   Angle at which halftone dots repeat. In black-and-white reproduction, 45 degrees is the best angle for producing the illusion of grayscale.

selection area   The selected portion of the image that will be scanned and saved to a file, copied to the clipboard, or printed.

shadow   The darkest part of a continuous tone or halftone image. The range between highlight and shadow determines the range and the differentiation of grays in the image.

Sharpening   A DeskScan II option that emphasizes detail by increasing the contrast of the boundaries between light and dark areas of an image.

TIFF (Tagged Image File Format)   An industry standard image file format supported by many applications.

TWAIN   An industry standard software interface standard developed by Hewlett-Packard and other hardware and software manufacturers. Used to scan images without the necessity of leaving the software application being used.

vector graphic   Images consisting of straight or curved line elements. Vector images can be enlarged or reduced without losing resolution.

Windows Bitmap   A bitmapped graphics format developed by Microsoft for use with Microsoft Windows applications.

Zoom   A feature of the DeskScan II software that provides the ability to enlarge a view of an image in the Preview area.

INDEX

COLOPHON

Super Scanning Techniques was produced electronically with Hewlett-Packard Vectra 486 computers. Body text was typeset with Adobe Garamond; chapter and section headings were set with Adobe Futura Condensed. Microsoft Word for Windows 2.0 was used for text preparation; pages were formatted with Ventura Publisher 4.1. All images were scanned with HP ScanJet scanners and HP DeskScan II software. Scanned images were edited or modified with Adobe Photoshop 2.5 or Aldus PhotoStyler 1.1a. Special effects were added to some images with Aldus Gallery Effects or Adobe Photoshop 2.5. Traced images were produced with Adobe Streamline 3.0 or CorelTRACE. Adobe Illustrator 4.0 or CorelDRAW 4.0 was used for editing of traced images. Illustrations of computer screens were captured with Inset Systems Hijaak PRO 2.0. Page proofs were produced with a Hewlett-Packard LaserJet 4M 600 dpi laser printer. Plate-ready film was produced on a Monotype™ imagesetter. This book was printed by Haddon Craftsmen.